A TOXIC SOCIETY

Abuse Of Power

RAE STANLEY

EDITED BY EMMA RALPHS

Publishing and Copyright

© Rae Stanley 2023

The Author asserts their moral right to be identified as the Author of the work. All rights reserved.

To the maximum extent permitted by law, the author disclaims any and all liability in the event any information, commentary, analysis, opinions, advice and/or recommendations contained in this book prove to be inaccurate, incomplete or unreliable, or result in any investment or other losses. Although the author and editing team have made every effort to ensure that the information in this book was correct at press time and while this publication is designed to provide accurate information in regard to the subject matter covered, the publisher and the author assume no responsibility for errors, inaccuracies, omissions, or any other inconsistencies herein and hereby disclaim any liability to any party for any loss, damage, or disruption caused by errors or omissions, whether such errors or omissions result from negligence, accident, or any other cause.

A full bibliography of where data has been gathered via the extensive research can be found on www.raestanley.com under the book title page.

Published; Oxford, United Kingdom

24th November 2023

Printed by Amazon Italia Logistica S,r,l

Torrazza Piemonte (TO) Italy

ISBN 9798866320653

Chapter Index

Preface

Chapter 1

Western War Crimes by Heads of Nation And Amendments to International Humanitarian Laws

Chapter 2

The Rise of Adolf Hitler and Nazi Ideology

Chapter 3

Abuse of Religious Power

Chapter 4

Institutional Racism, Police Brutality and Civil Rights

Chapter 5

The Abuse of Power in Trusted Positions of Authority

Chapter 6

Issues of Power and Misrepresentation in the Media

Chapter 7

Hate Crimes against Muslim Communities

Chapter 8

White Terror Influence Groups

Chapter 9

Mass Murders and the power of 'Blurred Lines' justice

Final Thoughts

Acknowledgements

Many people are to thank for their help in writing this book. Firstly, the amazing Emma Ralphs, who I cannot thank enough for her thoughtful and thought-provoking insights, her impeccable use of the English language and the ability to understand what I really mean when I can't find the right words. Emma, you are a star, and an angel and I will forever be grateful to you.

Secondly, my tutors at Ruskin College Oxford. Bal, MG, Steph and Sasha. You showed me what life is like for others without my white privilege blinkers on back in 2015 and began my never-ending journey in an obsession with social policy, oppression and behavioral science education. Many of your words and lessons will stay with me for life and I am really proud to have been one your students.

Finally, family and friends. For being you. For being supportive. For believing in me when I couldn't, filling me with courage and strength, and for building me up when I thought I was sinking. My children, all of whom I love dearly and now my little baby grandson too. And last but not least, my husband. For helping me to be my best, for being an amazing husband, my protector, my rock, my safety net and my all-time best friend in the world.

Preface

This book is a select, and certainly not a complete, compilation of events, people, and situations from around the world where 'power' has been destructive and, on many occasions, led to acts of terror. Our focus is Western society and capitalism, starting with the diverse types of power found and how they emerge from the top classes down to the lower classes. We will look at a sort of pyramid shape which describes how power is mostly held in the smallest section of the society - the upper classes. As you move down the chain of command, power decreases, with the bottom of the pyramid having the least amount of power and where the most amount of people are.

Where someone is located on the pyramid is informed by factors such as their title, qualifications, employment status and role, and their socio-economic status. Those at the very top benefit from those below them in the pyramid. They tend to be the policy and law makers. While those at the bottom rely on the decisions that are made by the top.

Power is desirable. With power, usually, comes money, property, respect, status, and security. Often it brings decision making responsibilities. The 'survival of the fittest' no longer works as it does in the animal world. Human beings around the world are held 'ransom,' not by strength in the physical sense but because of their strength of the voice, ancestral wealth, or power. A person's societal status can make or break them.

French and Raven's 'The Five Bases of Interpersonal Power' model (see the diagram below) sets out the different variants of power and how they are acquired. Michel Foucault theorized that power is constituted through accepted forms of knowledge, scientific understanding, and accepted discourse, known as 'truth,' which is used to construct society and maintain the desired status quo. Power is most visible to those against which it is used. In this book, we will explore various instances of the abuse of power in the disproportionate deaths, inhumane treatment, degradation, and the use of excessive force and violence against marked groups of people.

The Five Bases of Interpersonal Power

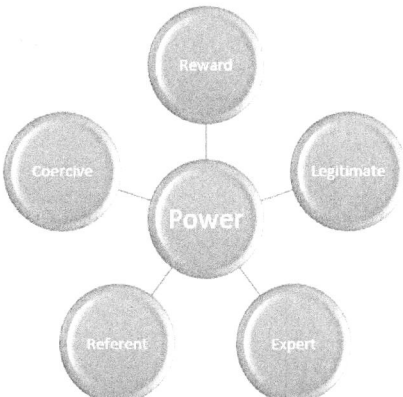

French and Raven 1959

Legitimate Power

In French and Raven's 'The Five Bases of Interpersonal Power,' the concept of legitimate power is the type of power where someone with authority can command, lead, and take charge of other people. For example, a parent has legitimate power over a child, taking responsibility of them and making decisions for them; a religious minister is granted legitimate power by their position; a country's leader has legitimate power its citizens.

Legitimate power is used (and abused) in matters of war and peace; life and death; freedom and imprisonment.

In countries that are, and have always been, predominantly white, the theory of white privilege plays an important part in obtaining legitimate power. Through racial prejudice and the belief that one race is superior, this 'superior' race obtains legitimate power. For example, colonizers forced native people to learn English and change their cultural beliefs to adhere to their way of life. The view that one race is more educated, intelligent, trustworthy, and 'right' than another race creates legitimate power. This form of legitimate power becomes a point of contention for both the oppressed and the oppressor. For example, when this status quo is challenged, and particularly when moves towards inclusivity are made, the oppressor may express concerns of being 'taken over,' which often stems from a fear of change and loss of control. Extremist views and xenophobic reactions often arise from this fear of being 'taken over' and marginalized.

Expert Power

Expert power comes from experience, education, and perceived expertise. For example, the reputation of certain academic institutions grants expert power. Graduates from the Universities of Cambridge and Oxford are thought of as highly knowledgeable, especially in their chosen subject of study, which gives them expert power. A large majority of politicians are graduates from Oxford and Cambridge, as well as the London School of Economics and Manchester University, other reputable institutions. In the most recent election, many of those elected to Conservative Party seats were graduates from these universities. Expert power also comes from connections with others in the same field. It is not always what an individual knows but also who they know and who they are that can earn them expert power.

It may come as a surprise that many Members of Parliament (MPs) have not attended university. MPs are assumed to be knowledgeable, and there is the presumption that this can only come from degree-level education.

Referent power

Referent power comes from popularity. Anyone with a large following, who is respected, or well-liked by many, will be able to influence others. Leaders in their field, celebrities, entrepreneurs, organisations, especially charities, and even your local MP would have referent power.

Coercive Power

Coercive power is gained by threatening, manipulating, and inciting fear in others. Governments, legal officials, teachers, parents, and siblings can exercise coercive power. For example, an employer could coerce their employees into changing their hours, taking a pay cut, or taking on more responsibilities with the implicit threat that if they do not agree they might lose their job, which could incur further consequences.

Coercive power is most effective when other forms of power are present. For example, in a relationship, coercive power could mean that the person in control of the household finances exerts power against the other partner as a form of control. They can prevent the other partner from spending money, socializing, and being able to take control and leave the relationship. Coercive control has recently been defined as a type of domestic abuse and is now a punishable offence.

Reward Power
Employers and parents commonly use reward power to promote good behaviour. B.F. Skinner's operant conditioning model shows how positive reinforcement works as a form of power {reference}. Power is gained by withholding a reward when there is noncompliance. The other forms of power an individual holds contribute to the effectiveness of reward power.

Power Stacking
This is a simple look at the idea of 'Power Stacking' and how various aspects of an individual's life can increase or decrease the power they possess.

	Skin Colour	Nationality	Socio/Eco	Gender	Education	Religion	Job Title
1	White	British	Mid Class	Male	UK Degree or Higher	Christian	Royal Family
2	White	British	Mid Class	Female	UK Degree or Higher	Christian	Royal Family
3	White	British	Mid Class	Male	Higher Ed	Christian	GOV
4	White	British	Mid Class	Female	Higher Ed	No	GOV
5	White	British	Work Class	Male	Non-Higher	Christian	PC
6	White	British	Work Class	Male	UK Degree	No	PC
7	White	British	Work Class	Female	UK Degree	No	Headteacher
8	White	British	Work class	Male	UK Degree	None specified	Teacher
9	Black	British	Work Class	Male	UK Degree	Christian	Teacher
10	Black	British	Work Class	Female	UK Degree	Christian	Teacher
11	Black	Rwandan	Work Class	Male	UK Degree	Christian	Teacher
12	Black	Rwandan	Work Class	Female	Non-UK degree	Christian	Teaching assistant
13	Asian	British	Work Class	Male	Non-Higher	Muslim	Teaching assistant
14	Asian	British	Work Class	Female	Non-Higher	Muslim	Teaching assistant
15	Asian	Pakistan	Work class	Male	Non-Higher	Muslim	Shop worker

16	Asian	Pakistan	Work Class	Female	Non-Higher	Muslim	Shop worker
17	White	British	Work Class	Male	Non-Higher	No	Unemployed
18	White	British	Work Class	Male	Non-Higher	None specified	Unemployed
19	White	British	Work Class	Female	UK Degree	Christian	Single Employed Mother
20	White	British	Work Class	Female	Non-Higher	No	Single unemployed mother
21	Asian	Syrian	Work Class	Male	Non-Higher	Muslim	Asylum seeker
22	Asian	Syrian	Work Class	Female	Non-Higher	Muslim	Asylum seeker

The illustrated table shows how, in reference to French and Raven's power forms, 22 individuals from the UK would be ranked according to the forms of power they hold. The table is categorised by skin colour, nationality, socioeconomic status (class), gender, the highest level of academic attainment, religion, and job role. This list of variables is not exhaustive.

At the top of the table is the 'most powerful' individual. They are the 'model' British citizen: highly educated, British born-and-bred, middle-class, male, Christian, and is in an elevated position of authority. They could be in a high-level leadership role like the Prime Minister, or in a law enforcement role. This individual is white and male, which is a large contributor to the power they hold. The UK is patriarchal society which grants men more legitimate power than women. As a white male, in a predominantly white country, this individual will have more legitimate power. They are socially and economically stable and their role gives them further legitimate power. They have referent power from holding (or stating that they have) Christian values, as well as expert power from their role and education. Their career means they are likely to have a clear criminal record, gaining them additional referential power.

'Power banking' describes how a person's background, ethnicity, gender, race, sexual orientation, financial status, family arrangements, the company one keeps, and even appearance can allow an individual to build up the power they hold.

In the table, light pink areas highlight where 'power banking' can be beneficial. For example, even though women have less power than men in terms of gender, they can still obtain power through other factors such as their job or race. It is unlikely that in a demographically white country, a Syrian refugee with no economic backing, with children and with little education, would be able to obtain the same stack of power as a white British equivalent. A Syrian, Muslim refugee has little power, although as a man he would have a modicum of advantage over a female Syrian Muslim refugee in the same situation, particularly if there are children involved. Power imbalances are how social injustice can prevail.

The drawing up and legalising of social policies is undertaken by individuals (usually men) with a large power stack, like those in rows one and two of the table. Policymakers have little forethought, understanding, or empathy for those at the bottom of the table, which reinforces and perpetuates power struggles, class systems, and socio-economic diversity. Policies become sources of argument, and those that need policy changes the most are the ones with the least amount of power to get those changes made. This is where extremist views may begin to surface, particularly from dissatisfaction with governing bodies. Protests and riots often stem from feeling powerless and experiencing socio-economic difficulties.

In other countries around the world, the opportunity to power stack will vary, depending on the country's demographics, history, governing practices, religions, and cultures.

Power may be drawn or withdrawn based on an individual's criminal records, their credit score, residential status, postcode, if they have a disability, the languages they speak, their family's financial situation, their age and sexuality.

Around the world, the upper classes, government officials, members of the royal family, and others with highly influential powers have been involved in various criminal acts. This is an abuse of power and yet rarely seems to negatively impact on their power. Tax havens, drug use and other scandals seem to disappear over time without consequence. For example, The Panama papers exposed the fraud, tax evasions and offshore accounts of many celebrities, public officials, world leaders and multinational businesses. These types of dealings only serve to ensure that profit can be kept securely, with lower tax rates than the country in which they usually operate or live in, and therefore pay less tax than they would do here in the UK.

The privilege of the Law of Clemency

Presidents have the constitutional authority to grant clemency, pardon federal crimes, reduce sentences, grant exemption from punishment and overturn court rulings. A pardon from the president is effectively a 'forgiveness' for the crime. The accused will no longer be punished, nor can they be retried. The power to grant clemency can easily be taken advantage of and repeatedly has been. In 1865, President Andrew Johnson granted pardon to many of those who had joined The Confederate Rebellion. When individuals who worked in higher offices were not granted pardons, they applied directly to President Johnson. Those with money bought assistance from individuals who had direct access to the President. Many of the officials were pardoned and continued to run for office in the following election.

President Donald Trump used his clemency on 13th April 2018, to pardon former Chief of Staff to the Vice President, I. Lewis "Scooter" Libby of obstructing justice and lying to law enforcement during an investigation. In 2007, President George W. Bush had convicted Libby for the obstruction of justice and lying under oath for lying to the FBI. President Trump also pardoned a former sheriff after he breached a federal court order to stop racial profiling people of Latin American background.

In January 2021, before his impeachment trial and President Joe Biden's inauguration, President Trump pardoned 74 people. John Gramlich reported that, according to statistics compiled by Pew Research Centre, despite the large surge in clemency applications granted in his final days, President Trump granted clemency to fewer people in his four years in term than President Barack Obama. Trump granted just 2% of clemency applications in one term, compared to the 5% of clemency applications granted over two terms by President Obama. Throughout his presidency, President Trump has granted clemency to people convicted of drug trafficking, violence, possession of firearms, fraud, bribery, and security breaches. He granted pardons for crimes such as conspiracy and tax evasion, as well as armed bank robberies. These pardons were often for people in high-ranking positions such as CEOs, law enforcement officers, presidency aides, family, and family friends, and other 'allies' of the President. Power can be used for good. For example, to commute sentences, pardon people for crimes where the punishment has changed since they were sentenced, and instances where the accused has redeemed themselves through good behaviour. During his presidency, President Obama granted clemency requests for people who had been charged for 'acquiring and possessing food stamps in an unauthorised manner.'

Any abuse of power is dangerous. But especially when someone uses their position of authority to hide behind while they comprise the safety of others and protocol. When positions of authority are abused, it often means that innocent people die.

"We hang the petty thieves and appoint the great ones to Public Office" - Aesop

Chapter 1 - Western War Crime by Heads of Nations and Amendments to International Humanitarian Law in Response.

In this chapter the Geneva Convention is explained before Western war crimes are documented, noting their position with regards to timelines of amendments and humanitarian response.

At this time, September 2023, the most up to date Geneva Convention Laws apply when at least two of the parties involved in combat are bound by the Geneva Convention at the beginning of the conflict. The purpose of the Geneva Convention is to protect the victims of armed conflicts and consists of the following aspects:

To protect people, to prohibit effects including excessive loss and destruction, and to preserve life.

People, places, and equipment protected by the convention include, and are not limited to: Military medical personnel, religious personnel, civil defence staff, medical transport and equipment – provided it is used as intended and not as a rouse to enact a combatant attack - wounded military personnel in the field and at sea, prisoners of war and non-combatant civilians. The Red Cross and Red Crystal emblems are internationally recognised and are also protected internationally underneath the Geneva Convention.

The convention prohibits attacks against civilians which means that only military objectives are authorised to be attacked in combat. Weapons used in international dispute cannot be used to cause excessive suffering or unnecessary harm, including long term effects on the natural environment. It is prohibited to treat opposition civilians differently and subject them to harassment or violence.

The Geneva Convention was first implemented in 1864 to protect wounded and sick soldiers. Amendments to the original convention came after conflicts with significant combat evolution, mass loss and destruction. In 1906, The second Geneva Convention amended the provisions to cover military personnel at sea. In 1929, the amendments extended to include prisoners of war and prohibited any form of inhumane treatment. Following World War II, further amendments were made because of acts committed during conflict. The fourth convention readdressed and laid out the terms of the conventions that had been disregarded during World War II. In 1977, additional protocols were added to further protect combatants and civilians. Protocol II was added to address domestic and internal combat and conflict.

The actions of the West have attributed significantly to the additions to the Geneva Convention and other amendments to international laws.

We will look at a brief history of the rise of the Nazi party in Germany and the subsequent amendments to the Geneva Convention that were put in place to ensure that the crimes they committed would not happen again. However, we will first at the actions of the Allies in the West and the impact of their crimes.

Prime Minister Winston Churchill is still considered a national hero, a figure of victory and justice. His leadership throughout World War II earned him continued respect and loyalty from the British public. However, his racist and fascist actions prior to and during the war are lesser-known public knowledge.

Winston Churchill wanted an empire. He had colonial ideals and was a white supremacist. Some may argue that Churchill was not a white supremacist because he 'fought and won' the war against the Nazis. Throughout his life, Winston Churchill's actions and words indicated white supremacist beliefs, which were ignorantly fueled and supported by many in the West at that time. His involvement in conflicts in Afghanistan, Greece, Egypt, Guyana, Iran, Iraq, Kenya, South Africa, and Palestine were fueled by ideas of racial superiority and hierarchy. He was not opposed to using gases and chemicals in warfare and, as Anthony Audi stated in his article on the 25th of August 2016 ('*Men of Power and Their Obsession With Winston Churchill*, Literary Hub, 2016) was thought to be a 'ruthless man'.

The Bengal famine of 1943 – 1944, claimed the lives of reportedly three million people. At the time, India was under British rule. The famine began following a series of natural disasters. The actions of Prime

Minister Churchill only exasperated the famine. Some see it as mistake of priorities, and others consider it an act of imperialism and superiority. Produce was exported to Europe while the Indian population starved. Churchill allegedly commented that the breeding in India was the problem and not the lack of food.

Winston Churchill supported Palestine for the Jewish people. His 'White Paper' included a promise that the British owned Palestine would be a Jewish state but there was a limitation to prevent enforcing Jewish nationality on the Arab population. In 1947 the UN General Assembly passed Resolution 181 where Palestine was called to be partitioned into 2 states, 1 part Jewish and the other Arab. Conflict in Palestine/Israel has since been a violent and ongoing problem with many talks and agreements failing to produce results that satisfy both parties. Conflict has reached another high as it recently intensified drastically again in 2023.

In South Africa, Churchill's involvement came when he argued for Afrikaners' right to self-rule. Churchill supported the deputy leader of that Parliament, Jan Smuts, who passed the Land Act which prevented land being sold to African people from European countries. Smuts believed that South Africa should be for white people, and that Apartheid should be supported. In 1920, 1 year after becoming Prime Minister, Smuts passed a law of segregation of residential areas that segregated urban areas, although near the end of his career he supported recommendations to relax these laws.

In February 1942, **President Franklin D. Roosevelt** following the Japanese attack on Pearl Harbor in 1941, issued Executive Order 9066 that authorized internment and relocation of Japanese Americans. Tens of thousands of Japanese Americans were relocated, mainly from the West Coast, and detained in military internment camps. Roosevelt justified the order as a military necessity. In January 1944, the Supreme Court overruled the order, and the last internment camp closed in 1946.

During World War II, President Roosevelt denied help to thousands of Jewish refugees, including refusing to allow a ship of refugees to alight in the US. It was not until 1944 that he reversed this decision to help. The mistreatment of refugees during World War II largely stemmed from widespread national paranoia regarding spies. Refugee persecution is often justified as a necessity for national security. Many believe it has escalated further in society via technological advancements, information sharing, public domain and the media which has also led to an increase in Nationalist extremism public presence in the West.

In August 1945, President Harry S. Truman authorised the atomic bombings of Hiroshima and Nagasaki with an aim to force the surrender of Japan the nuclear bomb headed for Hiroshima weighted almost 10,000 tons. It was flown to Japan from the States by Colonel Paul Tibbets and Bombardier Thomas Ferebee was to release the bomb over the intended target. Hiroshima had not yet been subjected to an aerial attack and residents had become used to air raid sirens in the mornings from non-combatant American aircrafts flying overhead.

The attack killed more than 80,000 people instantly. More deaths followed from injuries and the effects of radiation poisoning. On the 9th of August, the US released a second nuclear weapon onto Nagasaki. Major Charles W. Sweeney discharged the bomb from a modified B-29 Bomber aircraft. The attack killed more than 60,000 people. The United States military were planning a third attack, but Japan surrendered unconditionally before it could happen. Their surrender brought World War II to an end. At the time, President Truman was not classed as a war criminal as the atomic bomb was a new form of weaponry and using it had not yet been classed as a crime. It was not until 1949 when the Geneva Convention added a protocol about weapons of mass destruction that they considered it as such.

In 1954, during President Truman's final terms, the US joined the growing conflict in Vietnam in response to the fear that Communism was spreading throughout Asia. On the 1st of June 1954, President Eisenhower set up the covert operation; The Saigon Military Mission to support South Vietnam against the North. However, by 1959, the Viet Cong (North Vietnam) were engaging in fire fights with the South Vietnamese army which started a war. In 1961, John F. Kennedy was elected as President, with Lyndon B. Johnson as Vice President. In November 1962, President Kennedy ordered the United States Air Force to launch 'Operation Ranch Hand' which was the defoliation and destruction of enemy food supply in Vietnam with the use of herbicides such as Agent Orange. More than 4.8 million Vietnamese people were exposed to chemicals in these attacks, which led to the death of more than 400,000 people.

In the Vietnam War, President Kennedy also authorised the use of napalm, a chemical substance that American chemist, Louis Frederick Feisser invented in 1942. The US had used it in Berlin at the end of WWII on the 6 March 1944, and in Tokyo on the night beginning March 9th, 1945, killing at least 80,000 civilians in one night. They had also used it in the Korean War. In Vietnam, the US released it from B52 bombers and in flamethrowers on the ground.

Over 10 years of combat, 338,000 tons of napalm were used in Vietnam.

Also, in 1968, the US General, William Westmoreland realizing that they were unable to compete with the Guerilla warfare of the Viet Cong, the US military then turned to destroying everything they could. Military leaders encouraged the soldiers with the promise of rewards, including promotions, for the greatest number of kills. They killed women and children as well as the enemy soldiers. Whole communities were targeted on search-and-destroy missions as well as air assaults, and incendiary devices. In My Lai, US military killed 500 civilians in less than four hours. Other assaults and operations became more murderous such as the 'Speedy Express.' General Julian Ewell earned the nickname the 'Butcher of Delta' following a large-scale killing operation. It is highly recommended that readers look at the work of Nick Turse who writes in detail about his own findings about Vietnam War cover-ups in his book 'Kill Anything that Moves: The Real

American War in Vietnam' as we move on to the next subject here.

In 2003, the US President George W. Bush and the UK Prime Minister Tony Blair authorised the invasion of Iraq. In 2004, UN secretary Kofi Annan declared that their invasion and entry into the Iraqi War was illegal because it did not adhere to the 1945 UN Charter that was set up following the Second World War. The UN Charter consists of a general assembly 193 member states. The security council must request recommendations to the general assembly for further action to other bodies within the UN.

Under the UN Charter, member states agree to fulfil the obligations of the charter which includes maintaining international peace and security, preventing, and removing threats to peace, attempting to settle international disputes, suppressing acts of aggressions or breaches of peace, achieving international co-operation and develop relationships, and encouraging the respect of human rights.

At the time, officials from the US and the UK were aware that the military invasion would breach the charter. US officials have stated that their actions were in 'self-defense' as Iraq was refusing to surrender the weapons of mass destruction that were allegedly being made there under the reign of Saddam Hussein. During the invasion, the US reportedly used a reformulated type of napalm which had been prohibited by the Pentagon. The decision on how to respond to the situation in Iraq was for the responsibility of the Security Council and not for the Governments of the US and the UK to decide upon. The subsequent lack of consequences faced by the US and UK raises questions about the future of international conflict under the UN Charter. Neither the US nor Iraq were parties to the Geneva Convention's additional protocol 1. In their paper 'International Humanitarian Law in the Iraq Conflict,' Dr. Knut Dormann and Laurent Colassis detailed how the invasion of Iraq and the occupation fare against the international laws. It is recommended reading for more detailed information.

In Iraq, the **Haditha Massacre** took place on the 19th of November 2005. It is believed that the Kilo Company of the 3rd Battalion, 5th Marine Regiment conducted the massacre in which at least 24 Iraqi civilians were killed. In April 2006, during the investigations, the Regiment's commander and two company commanders were put on restricted duties. Over a year later, in December 2006, eight marines were accused of involvement. Staff Sergeant Frank Wuterich was leading the marines at the time. He was charged with multiple offences including making false statements and unpremeditated murder. From photo evidence, investigators determined that five Iraqi men were killed by close-range gunfire. Testimonies were obtained from some of the marines in exchange for their individual charges being dropped. Some of the marines were later court-martialed including Staff Sgt. Wuterich. By 2012, all charges were dropped by the judge including the murder charge against Wuterich, which changed to 'voluntary'. After pleading guilty to a charge of negligent dereliction of duty, he was sentenced to just 90 days in prison, a drop in rank and lower pay. There were no further consequences for the marines involved in the Haditha Massacre.

Sgt. John Edward Hatley, *(part of the 'Leavenworth 10' – a group of military combatants currently serving various sentences in the maximum-security Fort Leavenworth prison for the service men convicted of committing crimes in Iraq)* was the First Sargent of First Battalion, 18th Infantry Regiment. He was convicted of the murder of four Iraqi soldiers. He, and two other soldiers, shot the Iraqi soldiers in the back of the head while they were blindfolded and handcuffed. A whistleblower exposed the incident which led to Hatley, and the other individuals being charged and convicted. At first, Hatley was sentenced to life with the possibility of parole. In 2018, he was denied parole. But it was later granted, and he was released in October 2020 after serving 10 years at Fort Leavenworth Penitentiary, Kansas. The United American Patriots continue to object Hatley's conviction. They believe he is innocent and support his campaign for a presidential pardon. In an article from the 23rd of September 2020, the UAP argue the other soldiers 'had taken pre-trial agreements in exchange for testimony' and that there was no physical or ballistic evidence of the crimes. However, this remains to be seen. It is important to include this case because even if the charges against Hatley, or any other convicted soldier, were ever proved to be false in the future, it demonstrates the immoral actions of combatant soldiers and the Military.

Corey Clagett is another member of the Leavenworth 10. They claim they have been punished for the unlawful commands of their superiors during an operation in 2006 in Lake Tharthar, Iraq, known as the 'Iron Triangle', led by Michael Steele. Orders were given to kill any combatant man in the area. Clagett claims that although he knew that the orders were unlawful, the fear of consequences meant that he felt compelled to carry them out. He murdered of three Iraqi men who were fleeing after being found in a house. Clagett pleaded guilty of murder, attempted murder, conspiracy, and obstruction of justice.

In March 2012, **Staff Sergeant Robert Bales** unlawfully entered the homes of three families and shot 16 villagers in the Panjwai district in Kandahar, Afghanistan. It is claimed that he acted alone and was wearing night vision goggles. He killed 11 members of one family including children. Neighbours said they heard helicopters that night. It is unclear whether they were part of ordinary operational overhead surveillance or if they were sent out to assist, or to stop the gunman.

In response to 9/11 attacks on the World Trade Centre, President George W. Bush established **the Guantanamo Bay** detention camp. *The New York Times* published the 'Guantanamo Docket' on 22nd September 2023. It claims that 780 people suspected of Terrorism charges have been detained since 2002 at the military prison camp in Cuba. 732 of those men were held for many years without adequate legal support in horrifying conditions have been released having not ever been convicted of a crime. 9 men died in the prison before any convictions. President Bush declared that the detainees would not receive prisoner of war status and that they were 'unlawful combatants.' This breached Article 5 of the Third Geneva Convention, because he declared them as 'unlawful combatants' before a competent tribunal determined otherwise. It is argued that because Guantanamo Bay is in Cuba it is not subject to US authority, even though the camp was controlled by the US President with the detainees held under the US decision.

In 2001, the US set up the Parwan Detention Facility at **Bagram Prison**. It was designed to be a temporary detention centre, but it was a place for the torture and indefinite imprisonment of Taliban, Daesh and Isil fighters, as well as innocent civilians. It was open for 20 years, where more than 5,000 prisoners were kept there at any one time. US subjected prisoners to 'enhanced interrogation' which involved acts of torture and violations of international law.

The US is under investigation by the International Criminal Court for war crimes against civilians in Afghanistan under the Rome Statute since 2003 after

Afghanistan ratified it. The United States have never ratified this treaty, however Article 12 of the statute states that the ICC's jurisdiction includes acts committed within the territory of states that have ratified the treaty, regardless of the position of the accused perpetrators. The US have since refused to investigate the allegations within their country's justice system, and therefore it is open for investigation by the ICC. President Donald Trump recently pardoned two US soldiers who were previously convicted of war crimes by US courts. It is unlikely that many of the perpetrators responsible for the tens of thousands of civilian deaths in Afghanistan will ever be held accountable for their crimes. This is due to the lack of sufficient evidence, the barriers to investigations and the time that the investigations would take to complete for each alleged crime.

Abu Graib Prison is another US prison under intense scrutiny for human rights violations and war crimes. It closed in 2014 but there are photos which show prisoners being tortured, with over 70% of those prisoners being incorrectly detained. Contracted interrogator Eric Fair has publicly admitted that he classes the actions he took part in as torture. He has written his own memoir, 'Consequence; a Memoir,' where he details his remorse for his role in Abu Graib prison. Fair described how prisons were subjected to sleep deprivation, prolonged standing, and forced to holding crouching positions as well as freezing conditions and a lack of appropriate clothing. He is also incredibly careful to note people's opinions of what classifies as torture will differ. But enhanced interrogation should be classed as torture. There have been very few prosecutions for the torture and violation of human rights. Officials have not taken accountability for sanctioning the use of the abusive techniques in the State coalition-led Iraqi prisons. Only 11 people have been convicted of the criminal acts committed at Abu Graib prison.

Since the Iraq war, there have been numerous allegations against the UK for accounts of abuse, torture, beatings, murder, and sexual abuse that have not been investigated. A video from 2006 shows British troops beating four Iraqi boys. Due to the statute of limitations regarding time frames that crimes should be reported in order to be investigated, nobody has been prosecuted. Out of 3,400 cases, Conservative Government has only addressed 20 of them. The **UK Ministry of Defence** has denied allegations that crimes were committed and then covered up.

There are multiple reports of allegations and cases with reasonable basis to believe that these were crimes of war. It is, however, difficult to detail these incidents of allegations and the possible evidence of those charges due to lack of allowed public coverage within the court. The Prosecutors Office issued a report that gives reason to believe that UK forces committed at least seven cases of murder; at least 54 cases of cruel treatment, torture, or outrages of personal dignity, and at least seven cases of sexual abuse including accounts of rape. The report explains how there is insufficient evidence to believe that the UK Government has not refused to investigate the cases and therefore the International Criminal Court has not been warranted to investigate these instead. Clive Baldwin, a senior legal advisor, wrote an article for Human Rights Watch that relates to the facts and understanding of the report (8th December 2020).

The rise in historic allegations and reopened investigations against personnel has led to The **Overseas Operations Bill** which gained Royal Assent in Parliament in 2021. The bill grants stronger legal protection for military personnel and military veterans against prosecution and repeated investigations of alleged crimes in conflict. Human rights groups have opposed the bill because it would mean that the military could be perceived as above the law. The bill consists of two parts: a triple sectioned process to measure the context and the decision to continue with investigation and a shorter statute of limitations (6 years) of allegations unless there was compelling evidence that would warrant an investigation. In the cases of psychological trauma and emotional abuse victims might not have the time to mentally and physically regain strength, courage, and dignity to bring their tormentors to trial.

Overall, allegations of war crimes committed by Western military forces and those with the power to command, are not given the required investigation that is deserved. The Overseas Operations Bill could therefore be argued that it further protects military operations from scrutiny in the event of alleged crimes against civilians and enemy combatants. Military and Government officials who have control of the military can assert that power to evade investigation and avoid consequence for breaking international conflict laws.

Chapter 2 –

The Rise of Adolf Hitler and Nazi Ideology.

The severity of the Holocaust is widely known and understood, as well as its association with anti-Semitism. We will first briefly look into the Nazi party's rise to power, the formation of Hitler's Third Reich, and the manifesto that led to the Second World War and from which today's anti-Semites and neo-Nazis take lead from.

This chapter also looks at those who deny or downplay the atrocities of the Holocaust - referred to as Holocaust deniers – by using survivor accounts, historians, and conspiracy theorists to discredit and dishonor those who were imprisoned during the Nazi reign.

We will also look at current neo-Nazi groups who endorse right-wing nationalist ideology and believe in the propaganda spread by the Nazi regime against the Jewish community and other minority groups. Neo-Nazis espouse white supremacy, support ethnic cleansing, and promote a racial ideology which echoes Hitler's 'Aryan Nation' ideals.

Nazis Rise to Power

Adolf Hitler was born on the 20th of April 1889 in a small town in Austria. He had early ambitions of becoming an artist but failed to get into arts school. He began his military career when the First World War broke out in 1914.

At the end of World War I, defeated Germany was forced to sign the Treaty of Versailles by the Allied forces (Britain, France, and the USA). Under the terms of the treaty, Germany had to drastically reduce its armed forces and remove any remaining troops from the Rhineland. Additionally, they were to make extensive reparations to the Allies, realign their territories and accept the blame for starting WWI. Some prophesied that the harshness of the treaty was likely to lead to resentment and economic trouble for Germany. Many of those who joined the Nazi party had a great distaste for the Treaty of Versailles and the shame they believed it brought upon Germany.

In November 1923, Hitler and other rebels were arrested following a failed takeover of the government. Inspired by Benito Mussolini and his fascist regime and dictatorship in Italy, the Beer Hall Putsch resulted in an armed confrontation with the police. Hitler was tried and charged with high treason. He served just nine months of a five-year sentence. During his sentence, he wrote his manifesto, 'Mein Kampf' ('My Struggle') which expressed his obsession with the Aryan race, racial purity, and his belief that surrounding countries should be part of a German empire. The national coverage of the Putsch led to an increase in support for the Nazi party during Hitler's time in prison.

Following his release, Hitler focused on reshaping the Nazi party. He set up the Hitler Youth program to influence young people with nationalist and anti-Semitic ideologies. He also formed his own security force, the Schutzstaffel Security (the SS). The SS were responsible for protecting the Nazi regime and enforcing racial laws. This would later include overseeing and orchestrating many genocidal acts conducted against Jewish and other minority communities.

In 1930, Germany faced a severe economic crisis. Hermann Müller dissolved the Reichstag leading to demands for a re-election. The newly elected Reichstag had a large representation of Nazi and Communist seats. In 1932, Hitler was appointed as Chancellor. His rise to dictatorship intensified in 1933 following the fire of the Reichstag, which the Nazis and the Nationalist German Peoples' Party coalition claimed to be part of a communist plot. The 'Reichstag Fire Decree' gave the coalition immediate powers to take any action to 'protect the people and the state.' With their combined nationalist views, the Nazi regime grew and began to suspend civil rights, implement anti-Semitic laws, prevent political opposition including anti-racism and black activism, and took control of the press.

The Night of the Long Knives took place between the 30th of June to the 2nd of July 1934. It came after the Enabling Act of 1933, which allowed Hitler to make new laws without challenge. The Night of the

Long Knives, saw the execution, without trial, of members of the National Socialist party who Hitler believed to be a threat to his rise to power.

In 1933, construction of Dachau Concentration camp began. It was initially intended to hold political prisoners, but during WWII it became a detainment camp for Jewish prisoners. It was orchestrated by Hermann Goring and Heinrich Himmler; the former was the minister responsible for the formation of the Gestapo - Hitler's secret police force - and the latter was the head of the SS.

On the 19th of August 1934, 17 days after the death of the President Paul von Hindenburg, Adolf Hitler and the Nazi Party came to power with an 88% majority vote and the support of the Armed Forces. As Fuhrer, Hitler renamed Nazi Germany the 'Third Reich' (Third Empire) and began to instate the laws of the Nazi regime. Propaganda continued to spread, the SS took on a stronger role alongside the Gestapo, and policing and security increased under the direction of Himmler and Heydrich creating a totalitarian state. Young people were indoctrinated into the Nazi regime as a hatred of Jews was spread through the Hitler Youth program and a new school curriculum. Against the conditions of the Treaty of Versailles, Germany continued with rearmament and remilitarization. In 1936, Hitler ordered military forces to reoccupy the Rhineland.

The Night of Broken Glass (Kristallnacht) was a profound event of terror in 1938, during which Jewish-owned shops, properties, and synagogues were destroyed and vandalised. Jewish men were arrested for the sole reason that they were Jewish.

In 1939, Nazi Germany invaded Poland, which led to the declaration of WWII.

The Genocide victims and Ethnic Cleansing Programme

{Writing about any systematic genocide or war atrocity requires extensive research. It is not feasible, nor necessary to examine the full extent of every incident in this compendium of white terror here. Instead, we will only focus on areas that are relevant to our study. Readers are encouraged to follow up with further reading on the incidents discussed here.]

Throughout Europe, Jewish people were persecuted for threatening the continuation of German purity, and other minority groups were also oppressed. The Nazis subjected Black people to revocation of their civil rights, labelling them as 'stateless negroes' on their passports regardless of their birthplace, as well as forcing them to be sterilised, and excluding them from society. The Nazis also persecuted Roma Gypsies and Jehovah's Witnesses for not having 'true' German blood. They were also subjected to the Nuremberg Laws (see below) and ethnic cleansing. The Nazi ethnic cleansing programme targeted those with mental illnesses, disabilities, those of Slavic descent and Soviet soldiers that had been taken prisoner during the war.

The Nuremberg (Nurnberg) Laws

'The Nuremburg Laws' refers collectively to two laws, 'The Reich Citizenship Law' and 'The Law for the Protection of German Blood and German Honor.' They were put forward by Adolf Hitler to the Reichstag on the 15th of September 1935. Under these new laws, the Nazi regime could categorise German citizens by their perceived 'race.' This included Black people and Roma Gypsies who the Nazis considered to also be racially inferior, denying Jewish people of their human rights, such as preventing them from employing German women under the age of 45 to work in their home, revoking their citizenship cards, and marking their passports with a red 'J' to indicate that they were Jewish. Relationships between non-Jewish Germans and Jews were forbidden. Any marriages that took place, were not legally recognized by the Reich, and would lead to criminal proceedings and imprisonment in work camps. The Nazis denied Jews from the right to vote.

Ancestry also came under scrutiny. If a person were found to have Jewish grandparents, they would be persecuted even if they did not practice Judaism themselves. The Nazis made being Jewish a matter of race rather than religion. On the 14th of November 1935, the Nazi Party created a legal definition of being Jewish, based on heritage and ancestry, which would allow them to legally persecute Jewish people. The law came into effect the following day. Allies of Germany followed suit and created anti-Semitic laws for their own countries.

Germany's allied countries:

Bulgaria, Italy, Japan, Hungary, Romania, and Slovakia

Countries that had been invaded, claimed, or occupied by German troops:

The Sudetenland (an area that had both German and Czech population, and eventually transferred to German ownership) Austria, Poland, Denmark, Norway, Belgium, The Netherlands, France, The Channel Islands, The Soviet Union.

This included detainment and forced labour camps, alongside Death camps. According to research compiled by Jewish Virtual Library, there were 25 main concentration camp sites. These can be seen on the map that is located in the US Holocaust Memorial Museum. These main camps had subcamps located in the surrounding area. Some camps had two sub camps while others, such as Auschwitz, had up to 41 subcamps. The Holocaust Encyclopedia (from the United States Holocaust Memorial Museum) states that there were 44,000 different camps in total, ranging from temporary holding sites, ghettos, incarceration and detainment camps, euthanasia sites, forced labour camps, and the 'death camps.' They were located across various countries of the Nazi empire and its Allied countries.

How did Germany control other countries and implement camps in those?

By 1945, Nazi Germany, with the support of Italy's Benito Mussolini and Japan's Emperor Hirohito, had invaded and taken control of over 20 surrounding countries. The existence and locations of the concentration camps and their sub camps have been confirmed by many leading historians, archaeologists, the liberators of the camps, the detailed accounts of

52

Holocaust survivors, and accounts from Nazi officers. Operating under the same Nazi ideology, the purpose and conditions of these camps were equally as horrific across all camps. Both physical evidence and testimonies corroborate the atrocities that occurred in these camps.

At the end of the war, the Nazis and the Axis alliance countries attempted to destroy evidence of the camps. What remains leaves extraordinarily little, if no, room for debate as to the validity of the Holocaust. Surviving evidence includes clothing, mass graves, Zyklon-B canisters, and remnants of crematories and chambers. Holocaust survivors and the deaths of those who died after release shows the extent of mistreatment. Survivors have also given harrowing accounts of the treatment they endured while imprisoned. If the evidence, and corroborating accounts show the very real existence of the Holocaust, then why is there debate or denial from some groups? Could this be attributed to continuing white supremacist and nationalistic ideology? More on this in Chapter 5 where we look at white supremacist groups and Holocaust denial in more detail.

Chapter 3 - Abuse of Religious Power

"Do not indoctrinate your children. Teach them how to think for themselves, how to evaluate evidence, and how to disagree with you."
— Richard Dawkins, <u>The God Delusion</u>

Any religious entity has 'legitimate power' and the individuals within the religious order - such as priests, archbishops, sisters, etc. - have 'referent power' that is assumed due to the position held: the power of a leader. As previously mentioned, parents, guardians and wider society have legitimate power over their children. Often, they will choose the relationship they want their children to have with religion.

For centuries, there have been many disagreements between religions, and the Roman Catholics and Protestants are no exception.

The church used to have a prominent position in society, and many aspects of daily life revolved around holy teachings. A country's laws, policies and other ruling decisions will be influenced by the state religion. It will be upheld by institutions such as schools, the media, and society.

Historically, those who have the power to prevent the expression of opinion and choices of others, such as heads of churches, the Monarchy, and parliamentary figures, have also decided how society is then controlled by the powers of religion. Furthermore, they can change what is to be believed to further their own agendas. This can be evidenced in the following examples of change since the 1500s.

In 1517, in Germany, Martin Luther, a monk and religious reformer, began to speak out against the Roman Catholic Church, and questioned the power they possessed over people and their intentions, but his objections were silenced. Luther was excommunicated and declared an outlaw by the Holy Roman Empire; Emperor Charles V in the April of 1521. Despite this Luther continued to translate the bible into German as at the time only Catholic Priests were able to do so, Luther believed that they perhaps had misunderstood the Bible. It took over a decade to complete. Following his death, the

Protestant Revolution, which began in 1517 after Luther had posted his ninety-five theses on the church door in Wittenberg, continued across the West. King Henry VIII of England had initially disapproved of Luther's work but came to support it at the time that he then fell out with the Catholic Church.

In 1525, Henry VIII sought to annul his marriage to Catherine of Aragon, his wife and the mother of their daughter, Princess Mary. When the Pope refused to permit the annulment, Henry VIII appointed his associate Thomas Cromwell to Chief Minister in the April of 1532. Cromwell, with Thomas Cranmer, arranged for Henry VIII to legally annul his marriage to Catherine in the May of 1533. Henry had already married Anne Boleyn in that January, having separated from Catherine in the July of 1531. In 1534, Henry VIII proclaimed himself as Supreme Head of the Church of England under the Act of Supremacy which broke ties with the Catholic church. Anne Boleyn gave birth to a daughter, Princess Elizabeth on 7th September 1533, but after another miscarriage in 1536, Henry VIII ordered her execution. 11 days after the execution, Henry VIII married Jane Seymour who gave birth to a son, Prince Edward, on the 12th of October 1537. Jane died a few days later from childbirth complications.

Around this period, William Tyndale, an English scholar, began to translate the New Testament and part of the Old Testament into English. He believed that it should be written in the spoken language of the country. He was against the Catholic Church and had previously refused to work for the King. The top spiritual leaders of the time were against Tyndale translating the bible. He was arrested for blasphemy, accused of being a heretic, and executed in 1536 in mainland Europe where he had fled to. His work was however included in *Matthew's Book* which was published in 1537. The King authorised the English Bible, called The *Great Bible* in 1539 and declared that it should be read aloud during church services.

In 1540, Henry VIII had married again. This time to Anne of Cleves whom he quickly divorced 6 months later on the 12th of July. On the 28th of July he then married Catherine Howard. However shortly after, he ordered her executed for treason for undisclosed previous sexual relationships. Kathrine Parr was his next, and final wife, marrying her on the 12th of July 1543, Henry VIII died during this final marriage on 28th January 1547.

His son, Edward, then became King of England. As the new Protestant King, Edward VI stripped all the churches of ornate details and statues; priests wore plain robes and could marry; Latin mass was no longer used; and the *Book of Common Prayer,* which was written in English, was used during services. Before Edward's premature passing, he ordered that the throne should be passed to his Protestant cousin, Lady Jane Grey, rather than his older, Catholic, half-sister Mary.

Following the death of her brother, Princess Mary gathered public and military support to take the throne. As a devout Catholic, Queen Mary I sought to return England to its former Catholic state and renew relationships with Rome. The second statute of appeal allowed Mary I to dispose of all Protestant legislature and to bring in the death penalty for anyone who denied Catholicism. During Queen Mary I's reign, many people were burned at the stake for crimes against the Catholic Church.

In 1558, Mary I died, and Elizabeth I came into power. As Queen, Elizabeth I sought to settle the religious quarrel and introduced the Elizabethan Religious Settlement that founded a harmonious co-religious state. Elizabeth, I became the Supreme Governor of the Church of England with a new Act of Supremacy taking force. In 1559, the Act of Uniformity was passed, making it mandatory to attend a weekly church service and follow the *Book of Common Prayer* or be fined for nonattendance. In 1587, Mary, Queen of Scots was executed for her part in a Catholic plot to assassinate Elizabeth I, the Protestant Queen. Before her execution there was some concern that Mary would be Elizabeth's successor, which would have led to religious turmoil as she would have wanted to reinstate Catholicism.

During her reign, Queen Elizabeth I had blocked the marriage between Thomas Howard, her great-uncle and the fourth Duke of Norfolk, and Mary, Queen of Scots and prevented a Roman Catholic uprising. Thomas Howard was imprisoned in a tower and was later executed for his part in the Ridolfi plot. Roberto di Ridolfi, Howard and Mary, Queen of Scots had planned to remove Elizabeth I and return England to a Catholic state under the rule of Mary and Thomas Howard. In 1603, after 45 years on the throne, Elizabeth I died and her nearest relative James Stuart, King of Scotland, came to the throne. James was the son of Mary, Queen of Scots, and James V, and was the great-grandson of Margaret Tudor, Henry VIII's sister. His reign marked the unification of the crown for Scotland, England, and Ireland.

The Gunpowder Plot took place on the 5th of November 1605. It was an attempt by Robert Catesby, Guido Fawkes (Guy Fawkes), and other conspirators to blow up the House of Lords and bring an end to the public persecution of Catholics.

King James I was on the throne at the time, and he was a Protestant. The Gunpowder Plot can be likened to a modern day termed failed terrorist plot. The plot to kill the Stuart King and blow-up Parliament was foiled after an anonymous tip off to Catesby's brother-in-law. Guy Fawkes was discovered lurking around below the House of Lords. 36 barrels of gunpowder were found beneath the building. The failed Gunpowder Plot is remembered every year on 5th of November. Following this, Catholic persecution worsened as stricter enforcement was applied as a result of Fawkes treason. As you can see from the Tudor and Stuart dynasty the public experience of religion was turbulent, free will and choice were not options, those in power decided how people could worship.

Abuse against Children within the Roman Catholic Church.

Reports of child abuse within the Catholic Church show horrific abuses of power. Powerful community figures and trusted members of society abuse their power by mistreating the most vulnerable and trusting members of society.

Allegations of abuse towards children, young people, and vulnerable adults from within the Catholic Church began to surface in the early 1980s and emerged as an official 'crisis' in 2002.

Many of the investigated cases of abuse were originally reported to higher ministers and officials, such as bishops, abbots, and archbishops, within the Catholic church, rather than being reported to the police. They were supposedly dealt with by those in higher positions at the time. Instances such as these will be referred to as 'cover-ups' throughout this section.

Canon law is the internal legal system of the Roman Catholic Church. Other churches will have their own version, although some also follow the Roman Catholic system. The legal system within the church differs from civil law. Any canon laws that are broken will be tried by the Church's judges, barristers, and juries.

Under Canon Law, priests who were reported for being sexually inappropriate or sexually abusive towards members of their congregation were often moved to new parishes as these allegations were dealt with by the church Parish Priest. The reports of these allegations were then either filed away or insufficiently recorded and were only uncovered when the documents were subpoenaed. It has been reported that in some instances even once priests were moved, they continued to abuse members of their new congregation. In 1992, the US Conference of Catholic Bishops acknowledged that various bishops had covered up cases of abuse (NPR News, April 2010). According to Reuters, The US Catholic Church has paid out 3.2 billion dollars in compensation to victims of sexual abuse, of which, 7.3 million dollars went to more than 70 victims in the state of Colorado (Coffman, K. 2020). Canon law does not supersede criminal and civil laws; therefore, claims of abuse should have been dealt with by criminal courts, rather than by canon courts.

In 2019, Pope Francis abolished pontifical secrecy: the previous confidentiality rules that had protected Church governance and hidden reports of sexual abuse (Nick Addison, 2020). By abolishing the pontifical secrecy and adopting practices including directing clergy to report suspected abuse as required by law, it removed issues regarding reporting and speaking out about abuse. There is no longer an obligation to remain silent about matters of abuse and reports and documentation are required to be shared for civil investigation. This facilitates co-operation with law officials when allegations have been made, and direct accountability for those who disregard the law, or fail to follow correct legal safeguarding protocol.

It is estimated that between 1970 and 2020 there were over 1400 complaints of abuse within the Church (Shirbon, E. 2020).
The 2001 Nolan Report and the One Church Approach for Safeguarding Children formalised the Church's policies and practices across most of the diocese and religious institutions in England and

Wales. In 2008, The Cumberlege Report released findings on the progress of the recommendations of the NR and OCASC on the training of the clergy and cooperation with the legal authorities. However, further changes are still needed. There needs to be a better understanding from leaders within the church of when they have failed victims of abuse.

The Archdiocese of Birmingham is an example of where the Church has covered up instances of sexual abuse. In the 1980s, Samuel Penney, the Parish Priest of Olton Friary, abused a child in his clergy. The victim's mother reported the abuse to the Vicar General, Monsignor Daniel Leonard. Penney was moved to another parish in Birmingham, but the abuse allegations were not fully communicated to the new parish, and he continued to be in close contact with children. In 1990, a victim came forward with abuse allegations dating back to the 1970s. The victim requested that Penney should have no further contact with children. Bishop Pargeter responded to the allegation and the request, promising the conditions would be met. In 1991, Penney was sent to a therapeutic centre exclusively for the clergy. He then returned to the Nechell's Parish in Birmingham where he abused another young victim, while he was a guest in the child's parents' home. Penney was sent to the Gracewell Institute for treatment and was arrested there.

There have been numerous cases of sexual abuse in Roman Catholic educational institutions. Again, these abusers were moved to different institutions instead of being charged or punished. For example, Nicholas White, a Geography teacher at Downside School, abused several of his pupils. He was banned from teaching geography to one of his victims but maintained a position of great trust the school and remained in close contact with children. After a period of living away following the allegations, White was allowed to return to Downside School. He continued to abuse other pupils and remained at the school for a further 11 years. His misconduct was only discovered during an audit of the school's records. In 2012, the headmaster at the time, Dom Leo Maidlow Davies, is believed to have destroyed several files. It is unknown what these files contained.

In 1987, Peter Turner, a teacher at Ampleforth College, admitted to having sexual contact with a pupil to the headteacher, but the police were not informed. Instead, he was moved to a new parish in Cumbria where he abused two more victims. In 2002, he was sent back to Ampleforth College to be confined in the Abbey. In 2005, he was arrested and imprisoned following the findings of the 2001 Nolan Report. Turner eventually admitted to sexually abusing 14 victims. Following his imprisonment, further victims came forward.

Both Ealing Abbey and St. Benedicts School covered up various reports of abuse, which have now been investigated by the Independent Inquiry Child Sexual Abuse (IICSA). The IICSA investigated the Church's use of language within reports and communications regarding sexual abuse incidents. It highlighted how words and phrases had been used to make situations seem less severe, for example, the term 'inappropriate behaviour' has been used instead of 'sexual abuse.'

Members of the Catholic Church that have sexually abused children, have also abused their trust, power, and duty of care. These acts of sexual abuse happened in churches, schools, monasteries, in the victim's own homes, and often under the guise of 'medical' or 'wellbeing' appointments.

There are many reasons why victims of sexual abuse may not report what has happened or is happening to them. For example, it may take a victim of abuse a long time to build up the courage to tell someone else about what they have experienced or are experiencing especially if the abuser is a trusted member of society. The fear of not being believed, feelings of misplaced guilt, or fear of the abuser may also prevent a victim from coming forward. When the abuse is reported to a higher authority and is brushed off or poorly dealt with, it leads to a further loss of trust in the authorities that are meant to care for and protect our society.

Abuse against Women and Girls in Ireland's Roman Catholic Magdalen Institutions

"Ireland's Magdalene Laundries were residential, industrial, and for-profit laundries housed in Catholic convents where, between the foundation of the State in 1922 and 1996 (when the last institution closed) an as-yet-unidentified number of women and girls were imprisoned and forced to carry out unpaid labour for the commercial benefit of four religious congregations. They did so under conditions of severe psychological and physical exploitation by the nuns in charge, including constant surveillance, physical and emotional abuse, enforced silence and prayer, invasion of privacy, deprivation of educational opportunity, denial of leisure and rest, and deprivation of identity (through the imposition of "house names", the cutting of hair, and the confiscation of personal clothing and its replacement with shapeless uniforms)."

Maeve O'Rourke, Ireland's Magdalene Laundries, and the State's Duty to Protect (2011)

The Protestant and Catholic churches set up The Magdalen Laundries to primarily help working prostitutes find alternative employment and reform their lives. Later, Catholic convent orders took on the laundries and they became 'asylums' for 'fallen women' - women who were classed as sexually deviant under the Catholic Church's oppressive ideology of sexual morality. There are few official historical accounts of the abuse that transpired at the Magdalen asylums and orphanages. Like the cases of Canon Law discussed earlier, the Catholic Church received the complaints internally and supposedly handled them. The Church has not made all its records available, so most of what we know comes from the testimonies given by residents of the institutional houses (James M. Smith). This section of the chapter focuses on eyewitness accounts, and evidence uncovered, rather than data and statistics.

James. M Smith in his *book 'Ireland's Magdalen Laundries and the Nations Architecture of Containment' observes* that the nuns who ran the institutions, and those who lived there, were "products of their society, a society defined by a hegemonic social control" (Smith, J.M, 2007). Maybe the sisters would not have viewed the residents of the Magdalen Institutions as sexually immoral, nor have abused those in their care, nor allowed any known abuse to take place without consequence if they did not live in a society 'defined by hegemonic social control.' As Smith states, this does not excuse the actions of the Church and the sisters. It does, however, help to identify the societal struggles of women, and how difficult it would have been for those girls and women to seek help and support, whilst in the care of the sisters, and after they had left.

At the time of the laundries, it was widespread practice to send away women who were in 'trouble,' and it was strongly believed that these women should serve penance for their sins. 'Trouble' would be defined as women who were seen as promiscuous, pregnant out of wedlock, women who had been sexually abused, women who were daughters of unmarried women. These beliefs were perpetuated by religious sermons and texts, and traditional songs. In instances of sexual assault, the woman was always to blame, never the men. This victim-blaming mentality continues today. The influence of the church and the patriarchal hierarchy of society, together with the perceived roles of women contribute considerably to the reluctance and inability of those women to seek help and justice. By the time women came to terms with what had happened to them and had built up the courage to bring a case to court, it would often be too late, and it would be dismissed immediately. This is still the case with many sexual abuse cases in the present day.

Life at the laundries was grueling. Once admitted, the women were not allowed to leave until their penance had been served, which was subject to extension. They were given new names, their hair was cut off, and they were made to wear a laundry uniform. Some women reported that their breasts were bandaged tightly so that they looked less feminine. Work in the laundries was hard labour and seemed never-ending. The day would start early, with prayers and mass before breakfast, which would be a small portion of bread and dripping. Work would then begin, the women were ordered to work in silence, laundering for the convent, local hotels, and businesses. Laundering included washing, drying, ironing, sewing and other needlework, and the work came in at an alarming rate. The women were also responsible for cleaning, maintaining the gardens, working in the kitchens, scrubbing the floors, making rosaries, and knitting. There would be a short break for lunch and 'recreation,' however the women were not allowed to socialise and were constantly under surveillance. Minor transgressions such as breaking silence or forming friendships were punishable. Work continued until late before supper, prayers, and then bed. Forced labour, isolation and food and sleep deprivation are human rights violations. There were severe punishments for attempts to escape. Even if a woman did escape, they were often reported or returned to the laundries by members of the public. It was rare that the women would send or receive letters and any correspondence would be read by the laundry staff. If they gave any indication of harsh treatment, the letters would not be sent out, and the author of the letter would be punished.

There are many victims of abuse and forced adoption within these institutions that will never be identified. In the case 'O'Dwyer vs The Daughters of Charity of St. Vincent De Paul & Ors,' O'Dwyer brought forward her case against the laundry. During her time there, O'Dwyer was raped and became pregnant. She gave birth to a son in 1969 who was put up for adoption without her consent. The court ruled her case as statute barred. There were a range of factors which could have overridden the statute barred limitation, but they could not be proven. For example, O'Dwyer was an adult at the time of the alleged forced adoption and therefore the adoption was not legally invalid. O'Dwyer was never reunited with her son as he sadly passed away in 2004. Every day, around the world, adoptions happen without the mother's consent. In *Banished Babies: The Secret History of Ireland's Baby Export Business,* Mike Milotte writes about the scandal behind nuns in the Catholic Church putting babies born to unmarried mothers in the laundries up for adoption. Milotte explores the failings of the church and the State in the scandal, including the nuns' blatant disregard for consent and also the laws concerning legal adoption. The accounts Milotte includes paint a horrific picture of how the Church treated unmarried women and their children.

The 2002 film, 'The Magdalene Sisters', written and directed by Peter Mullen, is a fictional story based on accounts of life at the laundries. In 2013, Bill Donohue, the President of the Catholic League for Religious and Civil Rights, condemned the film in an article titled 'The Myths of the Magdalene Laundries', stating that the abuse did not happen. He affirms that:

> "no one was murdered. No one was imprisoned, nor forced against her will to stay. There was no slave labor. Not a single woman was sexually abused by a nun. Not one. It's all a lie."

Later in the article, Donohue lists the examples of abuse that were categorised in the 2009 Ryan Report following the 'Commission of Inquiry into Child Abuse' and claims that there were no "serious violations". He argues that "being kicked" was not uncommon as a form of corporal punishment in "many" homes at that time. He inadvertently admits that the laundries were not models of best practice.

Donohue does not take instances of sexual abuse seriously, dismissing "kissing," "voyeurism," and "inappropriate sexual talk." Donohue also says that in the 2013 McAleese reports, not one woman used the word 'torture', and because the word had not been stated, then torture could not have happened. However, the acts listed in the report include torturous methods of punishment and degradation. For Donohue, the laundries "were a realistic response to a growing social problem", that social problem meaning the rise of prostitution. Donohue's claim that none of the women were sexually abused by the nuns, and that any sexual abuse they may have suffered would have been elsewhere is presumptuous. There is much that can be discussed here about the socio-economic issues that prostitution and sex work stem from. But should the men who used the services of sex workers be classed and treated as "fallen" also?

From many survivors accounts the women who lived in the laundries reported that they felt trapped there. These women had been sent into exile, away from their families and their communities. Their only option was to stay in the laundries. Society was built on Catholic ideals and made it impossible for these women to return to their homes, or to start again and begin the reformed life that the nuns insisted they should make for themselves.

The fear of shame and retribution made the women feel even more trapped and these feelings stay with women in many countries and cultures today. The Draconian Laws and the Old Testament passages that oppress Catholic women, such as the sin of abortion and sex before marriage, are no different to older beliefs that a woman's menstrual cycle was a sin from God, and that women deserved to be in pain during their monthly cycle and were forbidden pain relief. The belief that women were, and still are, inferior to men maintains the oppression of women. It is here, that I think it, is odd that Western society in the 21st century condemns other cultures for their beliefs about women and girls yet refuse to acknowledge the continued inequality women face within the Western world as well.

By the end of 2018, the Magdalene Restorative Justice Scheme had paid out over 33 million dollars in compensation to over 700 women who had worked and lived in the Magdalene laundries. The McAleese Report noted that although the state had some involvement, most of the responsibility fell on the religious orders that ran them. It stated that there were cases of involuntary detention and that there were failures to explain to the women the reasons for their requirement to be there, or how long they were to stay. The report highlighted that women were stripped of their identity, subjected to forced labour, with no pay, no education, and no contact with the outside world. Some women were humiliated and degraded. The report notes that a large majority of women did not experience these injustices, but it does not deny that atrocities occurred in the laundries, as Donohue does. It also should be noted that the institutional power that the Catholic Church has over its members, and the women in the laundries, means it is solely responsible for their welfare. If the church agrees that 'fallen women' need guidance and support and have taken on the responsibility to help them, then they are also responsibility for their welfare.

The High Park Magdalen Asylum in Dublin was run by the Sisters of Our Lady of Charity. On the 23rd of August 1993, the remains of 133 bodies were found in unmarked graves. It was found that 58 legal death certificates were missing. It was an offence to not report a death, and yet no record of these deaths was found.

In Tuam, County Galway, the remains of up to 800 babies and young children were discovered in a disused sewage tank on the remains of St Mary's, the Bon Secours Mother and Baby Home, which had closed permanently in 1961. It had been run by the Bon Secours Sisters who took on the former workhouse in 1925. Concerns had been raised about the conditions of the home including reports of malnutrition, high death rates, and overcrowding but there was no formal investigation. The building was demolished in 1972, and in 1975, two boys found a chamber on the demolished site that contained skeletal remains. There was no investigation into the site. The local community decided to create a memorial space for the burial site. It was only in 2012 when Catherine Corless, a local historian, began her research into the site of the mother and baby home including obtaining death certificates for the children of the home and cross-referencing these with local family cemeteries that it became apparent what had happened. Corless obtained a list of 796 officially recorded deaths at the home. There are plans to exhume the remains to identify those who lay to rest there. The Sisters of Bon Secours have reportedly offered to pay 2.5 million euros to the fund and have confirmed that they will contribute to the victim's redress scheme, Government is still in talks with the religious orders regarding the redresses.

On the 12th of January 2021, the IISCSA released a 3000-page report which detailed the findings of an investigation into the deaths of around 9,000 children in church-run 'mother and baby homes' in Ireland. Between 1922 and 1998, 14 homes and four country houses were investigated. The report raised concerns of unsanitary conditions. It listed that there was insufficient heating in the wards, baby dormitories, and sleeping areas. There were insufficient blankets and unsatisfactory bathing provisions. The establishments were overcrowded, understaffed and with high mortality rates. There was also a significant difference between the statistical data on infant deaths at these homes, compared with the statistics for infant deaths in Ireland and specifically Dublin city. Institutional medical officers blamed the deaths on the mothers' bad care, including lack of nutrition for their babies. This is a plausible explanation because the lack of food given to the mothers would have affected their milk supply, causing insufficient nutrition of their babies. However, this is not the only explanation. Taoiseach (Minister for Foreign Affairs) Micheál Martin gave an apology on behalf of the state to the victims and the surviving mothers and children who were failed, shamed, and blamed by the homes.

Sister Eileen O'Connor, the area leader of the Sisters of Bon Secours Ireland, also issued an apology on the 13th of January 2021 which addressed the lack of empathy and compassion in the burials of the children who died in the home at Tuam which was run by the Order.

The Last Magdalen Laundry closed in Ireland on the 25th of October 1996.

"You shall not hurt a widow or an orphan"
Douay- Rheims Catholic Bible
Exodus 22:22

"Those who can make you believe absurdities; can make you commit atrocities."
Voltaire, Questions sur les Miracles à M. Claparede, Professeur de Théologie à Genève, par un Proposant: Ou Extrait de Diverses Lettres de M. de Voltaire.

Chapter 4 – Institutional Racism, Police Brutality and Civil Rights

Author's note: Regrettably, there is so much that should be covered about the history of Black enslavement, ongoing inequality and discrimination. At the start of writing this chapter, the desire was to cover as much as possible, but the fact remains that it is simply impossible to discuss everything, and everyone, in the detail they deserve. Each of the incidents included is someone's story and through learning about them their lives will continue to be remembered.

This chapter will look at instances from the transatlantic slave trade through to the present day, in both the United Kingdom and the United States. Every day, across every nation, human rights continue to be breached. Before colonisation, slavery existed on a domestic level as people from the same nationality would enslave one another, that is certainly not being disputed. Today, there is still modern and transatlantic. In over half of the world's countries, although human ownership is illegal, there is no criminal punishment expoliting others into forced labour.

This chapter will look at the repurcussions of institutional racism. With particular focus on police discrimination and brutality and the number of deaths in police custody.

In 2019, it was reported that the United States and Canada have the highest rates of civilian deaths by police services (www.statista.com). England and Wales were seventh on that list. In some states in the US, up to 88% of people killed by police were Black. In the state of New York, where Black people make up approximately 50% of the state's population, the number of Black people killed by police was far higher than the number of white people. If the number of Black people was equivalent to the number of white people across a country, it would be clear how disproportionate these figures are. Deaths recorded per country are not a true representation of the proportion of the minority population, which masks the true extent of inequality and discrimination within the law faced by Black people.

Racial discrimination and violence against 'non-white' people was, and continues to be, part of a global white supremacist initiative created by and capitalised on by European and North American countries during periods of international settlement and colonisation, for the benefits of wealth, religious beliefs and power. The Western powers colonised countries and displaced people, empowering domestic slave traders to not only continue, but also took advantage of those who were already enslaved or at risk of being so, for their own gain.

The following timeline explores events that examine historical and continuing institutionalised discrimination towards Black people, the abuses of power by white people in positions of authority in both the United States (US) and in the United Kingdom (UK).

1600 – 1899

17th Century – This marked the beginning of European settlers forcibly taking Black people and putting them onto ships to North America where they were sold into slavery.

18th Century - Over six million African people were enslaved by the Western countries and made to work on the plantations in America, particularly through the Southern states as well as in the North. They were subject to horrific conditions and punishments under regimes of cruelty.

1808 - The **International Slave Trade** had ended but continued for those already enslaved. Many Black slaves were sold into domestic slavery positions in the South, forcing families apart.

1861 - The American Civil War broke out on the 12th of April between 23 Union states and the 11 Southern states known as the Confederate states of America. President Abraham Lincoln and the Union States of North America were against slavery, following a move to a more industrialised economy, while the Southern rebel states wanted slavery to continue so they could maintain their wealth from the sale of cotton produced under forced labour.

1862 - President Lincoln issued the **threat of an Emancipation Proclamation.** If the rebellious Confederate States did not realign by the 1st of January 1863, the military would be sent to free slaves in those areas of rebellion.

1863 - The **Declaration of the Emancipation Proclamation** came into effect on the 1st of January following noncompliance from the Confederate States. Many of those who had been freed from slavery then joined the Union's military action against the Confederate States. Around 38,000 Black people lost their lives in the conflict.

1865 – The American **Civil War ended** on the 9th of April following the surrender of all Confederate armies.

1865 - The Reconstruction period began. Laws and policies were rewritten to include those recently freed from slavery. During this time, segregation was legal in schools on the provision that they were providing equal education and opportunities. On the 18th of December, **the 13th Amendment** was introduced, abolishing slavery. Under the ruling, slavery and involuntary labour would only exist as forms of criminal punishment.

1875 - The Civil Rights Act was implemented. Under the Act, the states, and the laws they enforced, could not discriminate. But civilians still could. By 1883 it was declared unconstitutional.

1877 – The end of the Reconstruction era began with the withdrawal of troops from the Confederate States. Despite the apparent improvement in rights for Black people, there was an increase in the anti-Black movement. White supremacy groups were gaining traction. The Ku Klux Klan was increasing in numbers. Those recently freed from slavery began migrating West, to start new beginnings away from the Southern states that were implementing new laws and constitutions that embodied white supremacist thinking.

1882 - Immigration control laws began in the United States.

1896 - Jim Crow laws were deemed acceptable within the constitution, providing that they were implemented by individuals and groups. They were not laws of the states and could not be legally implemented by the state itself. However, individuals, businesses, and organisations could still actively discriminate against Black people by refusing to honour their rights.

1899 – The Supreme Court agreed that if an education were provided it could legally be racially segregated without being 'unequal', overturning the **1896** Separate but Equal Education ruling. The consensus among white people was that Black people should not receive an education as this would be detrimental to white 'superiority.' The possibility that Blacks people would want, and be deserving of, jobs higher than roles of servitude or labour was a threat to the racial hierarchy that existed in America.

Education was segregated, and despite having the same constitutional rights as white children, Black children were not given the same opportunities. Funding was disproportionality awarded, with schools for Black students receiving a far below standard of resources, space, and buildings. In **1910** only 2.8% of Black students were able to attend high school as there were only four Black schools in the South. Education and training, particularly in the South, were funded by philanthropists and centered around industrial training, manual labour, and positions of service (Klarman, M.J. 2007).

"Between 1882- 1951 approx. 3,438 Black people were lynched."

Ferris State University

1900 – 2000

The United States and The United Kingdom

In the early 1900s segregation deepened throughout America and the oppression of Black people intensified. The racial divide was purposeful and obvious despite the 'equality' promised to all under the American Constitution. Barriers for Black people to voting, education, jobs and a decent standard of life were becoming increasingly obvious. The **Great Migration** period saw a wave of African Americans move away from rural areas to the industrialised cities to fill the vacancies left by those enrolled to fight in the First World War.

1905 - The UK government introduced the Aliens Act. This addressed nationality registration and gave the Home Secretary overall responsibility for matters such as immigration.

1917 (UK) – During the First World War, the British West Indies Regiment (BWIR) was set up within the British Army as a labour unit. It was formed of recruits that had been transported from the West Indian British colonies and enlisted as soldiers for the British Army. However, they were not granted the same opportunities to fight, nor treated as equals to white soldiers. These soldiers played a large part in manual labour duties such as trench digging, ammunition carrying, as well as ship and rail unloading. The work was dangerous and conducted treacherously close to opposition lines. BWIR soldiers worked and fought on the frontline. They were awarded medals for their bravery. They were also responsible for defending the war front in East Africa, which was occupied by the Germans. Initially, Black soldiers were not given the same pay rise that their white counterparts had received. It was only when fellow soldiers and neighboring governments protested that the raise was implemented. Following the war, Black soldiers felt resentment towards the UK as, despite fighting for it, its laws and people continued to discriminate against them.

1918 - **The First World War** came to an end. On returning home, white soldiers discovered that their jobs from before the war had been filled during the Great Migration. Black soldiers who had participated in the American war effort, returned to the United States to discover that their rights were no better than before. Jobs were scarce and white applicants were favoured over Black applicants.

1919 (US) – The **Red Summer began following** the death of an African American teenager in Chicago. A group of white teenagers threw stones at him as he swam in the lake for coming too close to the 'white-only' beach. This resulted in him drowning to death. Witnesses who saw the incident identified the attackers, but no arrests were made. The injustice of the incident and the lack of consequences for those who had committed the crime sparked a series of riots and protests. During the first riot, over 1000 Black families lost their homes and over 500 Black people were killed or injured. The very idea of equality remained a point of constant tension and violence.

1919 (UK) - Race Riots broke out throughout the country, fueled by hatred and discrimination. Like the US, the UK was facing an economic downturn. Industries that had shut down or taken a hit during the war were struggling and unemployment was rising. White people blamed Black people and immigrants for the lack of work in the cities and ports. Unions held meetings that were fervently anti-immigrant. Black people were targeted, abused, and attacked. There was growing anger toward inter-racial couples, particularly against Black men in relationships with white women.

In Liverpool, one of the areas hit hardest by riots, a young man named Charles Wootton, a naval firefighter, was killed. Following a fight, police officers began to discriminately arrest Black bystanders, whether they were involved or not. Charles Wootton was killed while attempting to escape. His murder was never investigated, and nobody was charged. In a brief court case, Wootton was described by the court as someone who had evaded lawful arrest and died in the process of escaping. The *Bradford Daily Telegraph* reported the case in a short article and declared it as an 'Open Verdict' on Friday 6th June 1919.

Following the incident, over 10,000 white people searched the city, attacking any Black person they found. Black residents had their houses looted and burnt down. Retaliation from Black people resulted in their arrest. Many Black men were fired from their port jobs, and many sent back overseas.

Following the incident, over 10,000 white people searched the city, attacking any Black person they found. They looted and burned down their homes. Police arrested any black person if they retaliated. Many Black men were fired from their port jobs, and many were sent back overseas.

The UK government passed the **1919 Aliens Restriction Act.** This was a continuation of an act through World War I that assisted in identifying enemies in Britain. It meant that foreign nationals had to register with the police, be restricted in their residence and also could be legally deported if so desired.

1920 (UK) – The Aliens Restrictions Act was amended to include the Aliens Order which ruled that Black and Asian people had to register with the police if they were searching for a residence or employment. South Asian people were exempt due to their contribution to the British Empire however they were very often caught in the crossfire as identity documents were not provided to prove that they were not 'aliens' to the country.

1925 (US) - The Ku Klux Klan had over three million members in the US, mostly from the Mid- and South-West states. In Washington DC, 35,000 members marched in protest of Black people's requests for equality.

The 1940s (US AND UK) - Black people migrated to the cities to fill the vacancies left by those recruited to fight in the Second World War. Housing was scarce and discriminatory practices such as 'zoning' which consisted of creating white-only or black-only areas were increasingly common in the 40s. These practices have had a lasting impact on both the demographics and 'worth' of areas causing continued segregation in the West. It has been argued that it is a matter of class or wealth rather than race. But ultimately, all these issues are linked. Black people were rarely part of the middle class; making up a sizable percentage of the lower classes that kept them from more affluent areas. By living in the deprived areas, loans were unattainable, which meant that they were financially trapped in these areas. The legal practice of zoning and denying financial requests based on where you lived continued through to the 1970's and continues to impact today's society.

1945 – 1949 (US) - Around 1,150,000 Black men were inducted into the military.

1948 (UK) – There were further large-scale racist attacks. The now named 'Windrush Generation' (named after the 'Windrush' Ship they were brought to the UK on) were brought to the UK to fill the vacancies left following World War Two.

1949 (US) – The President, Harry Truman, passed a housing act for white people. This was in response to the Supreme Court ruling that Black people could move into any property that they could afford to purchase. The housing act put Black people at further disadvantage, and white people more advantaged.

1954 (US) – Racial segregation in schools became a topic of discussion. Local courts were now responsible for deciding whether schools in their state would remain segregated. This was another opportunity to create a division between areas and schools within those specific areas.

In the UK, despite there being no official segregation of school children, the variation of housing opportunities was causing segregation.

1955 (US) - On the 28th of August, two white men lynched Emmett Till, a 14-year-old boy from Chicago, following allegations – which were later to be found false - that he had touched a white woman. Till was visiting family in Mississippi and had gone to the local shop with his cousin, Simeon Wright. He had whistled at the white female cashier as she went to her car. Two men from the woman's family kidnapped Till and brutally beat him. They then shot him before throwing him in the river using barbed wire to attach his body to a large cotton gin metal fan (shown in the image below). He was beaten to the point of being unrecognisable, but his mother was able to identify him by his ring. His cousin had seen the men as they came to kidnap Till and identified them to the police. Roy Bryant and J.W. Milam were accused of the murder of Emmet Till. However, after a four-day trial, the all-white and all-male jury, made up of residents from an area known for its racist views, acquitted both Bryant and Milam of their crimes in just over an hour. They were never convicted of the crimes and were protected by the Double Jeopardy law which prevented them from being tried again. Emmett Till's killers were paid $4,000 for their confession story by 'Look' magazine in which they described exactly how they had beaten and killed him and told of their concern for the safety of white supremacy in their state.

1955 (US) – In Maryland, a law was passed making it illegal for a white woman to give birth to a mixed-race child. The punishment was five years imprisonment. By 1957, it had been overturned.

1956 (US) - The Montgomery Bus Boycott led to the end of segregation on buses. It started with the arrest of 15-year-old Claudette Colvin for refusing to give up her seat to a white person, followed by the arrest of Rosa Parks for the same reason. Initially, the leaders of the movement had wanted equality for the back half of the buses where Black people sat. But the boycotts meant that buses lost 75% of the passengers which had a deep economic impact on the bus companies. Eventually, the courts ruled that buses should not be segregated at all as it was a breach of the 14th Amendment to the US Constitution.

During this time, Martin Luther King Jr becomes a more prominent civil rights leader.

1958 (US) – In Mississippi, Clennon King, a young Black man, attempted to apply for university. However, when he arrived to register, police officers arrested him. During his trial, the judge declared that

King was clinically insane, and he was admitted to an asylum.

1958 (UK) - The politician Oswald Mosley and various others argued that people who had been brought to Britain, such as the 'Windrush Generation', should be repatriated. During this period, Black people were subjected to frequent violent, racially motivated attacks including the Notting Hill race riots.

1959 (UK) – On the 17th of May, in Ladbroke Grove, near Notting Hill, London, a gang of six white men murdered Kelso Cochrane. There were witnesses to the attack, but nobody came forward and identified the attackers. The prime suspect, Pat Digby, and the other suspects were kept in neighbouring cells in-between being questioned by police, giving them adequate time and opportunity to corroborate their stories. There were rumours that the weapon Digby used to stab Cochrane was still in his possession, but the police did not search his home. Despite being asked to reopen the case in 2003 by Cochrane's brother, police did not do so and claimed that the evidence was no longer available. Kelso Cochrane's killer has never been brought to justice.

1963 (US) - There was a rise in Southern white supremacist group both in popularity and in action of attacks on Black communities, including the targeting of Martin Luther King Jr., his family and close community. President John F. Kennedy was considering reinstalling troops in the South and feared another civil war. Segregationists in the South opposed Kennedy's vocalised ideas for racial progression. After the assassination of John F. Kennedy, Robert Kennedy and officials refused to allow an addition to the Civil Rights act that would protect Black people from police abuse and abuse in custody. It was deemed that it was the responsibility of local police departments. Many states opposed the civil rights bill being proposed. Without full government backing against brutality towards Black people, they were unprotected by the constitution.

1963 (UK) -18-year-old Guy Bailey was turned away from a job interview at the state-owned Bristol

Omnibus Company. The manager told him that "we don't employ black people". This sparked the Bristol Bus Boycott which highlighted the continuation of racial discrimination. The protest received support from Church groups and various politicians.

1964 (US) - President Lyndon Johnson passed the Civil Rights Act which had started under John F. Kennedy's presidency. Johnson had been known to side against Civil Rights, but this changed in the run up to the election following Kennedy's assassination. The Act mean that employers could no longer discriminate against applications based on skin colour and ended segregation of public places including schools. It took a long time for this ruling to take effect and the desegregation of schools was particularly challenging. Around this time, test scores were introduced into schools to keep track of learning and rates of intelligence. These tests scores were considerably lower for those in black majority areas, highlighting the impact of unequal education and opportunities in the 1960s. The divide in educational achievement contributes to ongoing inequality in life goals and careers. Although now legally, Black people could not be turned down from a job based on their skin colour, the quality of their education, social status and its impact on learning and subsequent exam scores contributed to an unfair disadvantage when it came to applying for jobs.

1965 (US) – Martin Luther King Jr and other activists focused on ensuring that Black people were registered to vote and knew the importance of their votes. The Black Power movement grew, which focused on bolstering racial pride and self-determination in Black communities. They encouraged a distrust for white institutions.

1965 (UK) – The Race Relations Act was the first piece of legislation in the UK to address the prohibition of racial discrimination. The Act banned racial discrimination in public places, but it did not address discrimination in housing and employment.

1966 (US) –The Black Panther movement formed to protest and challenge police brutality towards Black people. They began to act following the assassination of Malcolm X, and the murder of an unarmed teenager, Matthew Johnson, who was killed by police in San Francisco. Their Ten-Point Program set out the goals and ideals of the party including demands of equality across society, an end to police brutality, the right to a fair trial with a jury of their peers (just as white people had) and an end to white power mentality and white supremacy. Today, the legacy of The Black Panther movement continues to be a source of empowerment for Black people in their fight for social and economic equality.

1967 (US) – Riots broke out in Detroit. The predominantly Black areas were struggling. During a period of financial inequality, there were continuing discrepancies in the standards of living, worsened by the benefits continuously awarded to the predominantly white and well-off areas.

Around 60,000 Black people were living in Detroit. Their homes were small and crowded together – which created conditions comparable to a detainment camp. They were subjected to far lower pay, high unemployment rates and poor living conditions. Businesses moved from the area to more 'profitable' white areas, leaving many Black residents without jobs. White people also moved away. The riots that ensued were in protest to the growing inequalities and to fight to be granted the same opportunities as white people. A predominantly white police force responded with brutality, leaving Black residents feeling vulnerable. The police would stake out certain establishments, which attracted groups of onlookers who waited to see what would happen. On one occasion a riot ensued: known as the 12th Street riot. It has been claimed that this was the third most deadly riot in America, with 43 people killed during the four-day riot. All social control services were deployed to control the situation and army troops patrolled the streets to keep the order. Fires broke out, making 5,000 people homeless and destroying 1,000 buildings.

In addition to the violence in Detroit, in New Jersey white police officers beat a Black taxi driver to death, sparking similar uproar and violence between Black people and the police force. A further 26 people died.

1968 (US) - Alongside amendments made in the UK under the Race Relations Act, in the US the Fair Housing Act was included under the Civil Rights Act. Highly populated black- majority areas were experiencing the ongoing effects of inflated house prices, unemployment, educational underachievement, and high crime levels which had been highlighted in the Detroit riots in the previous year. The Fair Housing Act was to prevent discrimination in gaining housing.

The Black Panther Party was evolving and becoming more influential among the Black communities.

Police shot a 17- year- old unarmed boy, Bobby Hutton, ten times as he attempted to escape his home that had been set on fire. Just two days before Hutton's murder, Martin Luther King Jr was assassinated. Politician Robert Kennedy, who had been supportive of the Civil Rights movement, was also assassinated. Before these incidents J. Edgar Hoover, the director of the FBI, ordered the FBI to eliminate leaders of the growing anti-fascist groups with misinformation, sabotage and use of lethal force. A period of destabilisation designed to divide and discourage any union through systematic and immoral acts began.

1969 (US) The Black Panther Party, fed over 10,000 school children everyday with their nationwide free breakfast for school initiative. Hampton, the leader of the Illinois contingent of the Black Panther Party, was instrumental in the initiative. He also set up free health programs and offered support for Black gang members to help them direct their frustrations elsewhere. Hampton's Chicago party rapidly grew in followers. Chicago police raided Fred Hampton's apartment, where he and four other Black Panther Party members slept. Hampton was shot four times, killing him while he slept. Officers shot Hampton four times, killing him as he slept. Other members of the party were killed or injured, including 17-year-old Mark Clark. Hampton's pregnant wife was also shot but survived.

The surviving members were arrested for the attempted murder of the police, despite only one of the 90 bullets shot being from the gun of a Black

Panther Party member. No police officer faced charges for the murder of the men who died, or the people injured. In the following years, the Black Panther Party disbanded due to the interference from the FBI, constant attacks, and murders of members which forced remaining members to flee the state.

1972 (US) – The Tuskegee study of 'Untreated Syphilis in the Negroe Male' finally ended. The study ran from **1932** and was an uninformed and unethical experiment on Black men. After being invited to a test to rid them of 'bad blood,' the participants were injected with the venereal disease syphilis without their knowledge or consent so the effects of untreated syphilis could be studied. Over 399 Black men were injected. As they were unaware that they had syphilis, they were therefore also unaware that it could be transmitted to others. After the initial study period, it was decided that all treatment would stop, and the men would be monitored until their death for results of the study. Some of the treatments prescribed included mercury and arsenic, but the antibiotic (penicillin) that was commonly used to treat it was not offered. Doctors were enlisted and told not to treat for syphilis. The long-term effects on the organs, brain and mental health of the participants led to a great deal of pain and suffering, and eventually death.

1981 (US) – Thirteen teenagers were killed in the New Cross Fire Massacre. It was an arson attack believed to have been carried out by a white supremacist group called the National Front. Police did not investigate the incident correctly. Protests were held and justice was demanded, however, no one has been charged for the crime. The police backtracked and said that they did not believe it to be arson after all. A further young boy who had survived the attack took his own life having fallen from the balcony of a block of flats after struggling to cope with what had happened.

1991 (US) – Four officers beat Rodney King as he was arrested for a drink driving offence on the 3rd of March. The incident was captured on camera (see image below). The officers tasered, hit King with batons and kicked him, which resulted in life changing injuries.

1992 (US) - At the trial for their attack of Rodney King, the four officers, Laurence Powell, Timothy Wind, Theodore Briseno and Stacey Koon, were acquitted of assault with a deadly weapon. The jury consisted of ten white people, one Hispanic person and one Asian person, there were no African American jurors on the bench. The LA Riots broke out on the 29th of March in response to the injustice of the police officers' treatment of Rodney King, and the substantiated belief that police officers unfairly racially profiled and acted with increased violence towards Black people. The National Guard was called in to assist in controlling the public and by the 4th of May, the riots had settled. Through a civil court suit, Rodney King was able to get justice for the breach of his civil rights against two of the officers and was awarded 3.8 million dollars from the state. Rodney King went on to write *The Riot Within: My Journey from Rebellion to Redemption* which was published shortly before his death in 2012.

1993 (UK) - Stephen Lawrence was just 18 years old when he and his friend Duwayne Brookes were attacked while waiting for a bus in Eltham in Southeast London on the 22nd of April. A gang of white youths murdered Lawrence in a hate-fueled, racist attack. A list of names of suspects was found left in a telephone box, but police waited four days before acting on this intelligence. In a conference with the Lawrence family, they raised concerns that the police were not doing enough to catch his killers which led to arrests being made between the 7th of May and the 23rd of June. Duwayne Brooks identified two of the attackers in an identification parade. However, his identification was deemed unreliable by the Crown Prosecution Service, and charges were dropped on the 29th of July. On the 22nd of December, the barrister claimed new evidence had emerged concerning the identification of further suspects and the coroner paused the inquest. In **1994,** the Crown Prosecution Service still refused to prosecute any of the suspects for the murder of Stephen Lawrence. In September, the Lawrence family took the three identified suspects through a private prosecution, bypassing the need for the CPS. In December, covert video evidence was presented, showing four suspects, including the three already identified, using violent and racist language. In **1996,** the prosecution failed again, and the three men who had been identified were now listed as 'not guilty' in the court records. The inquest into Stephen's death was resumed. By **1997,** there were now five identified suspects, but they refused to answer questions which halted court proceedings. The verdict was that it was an unlawful killing in an unprovoked racist attack. The following month, the Police Complaints Authority criticised police conduct in the investigation into Lawrence's murder. In **1998,** the suspects are given an ultimatum to either provide their evidence or to face prosecution. Stephen Lawrence's case and the courageous persistence of his family brought about the publishing of the Macpherson report that recognised the need for reporting and investigating incidents of racism, regardless of opinion. In **2002,** two of the suspects were imprisoned for a racial attack on an off-duty police officer. In **2004,** the CPS decided there was not enough evidence to charge anyone with Stephen's death. In **2007** the forensic team re-examined the case to look for new evidence using recent technology. In **2010**, one of the other suspects was jailed for a drug related charge. Finally, in **2011**, Clifford Norris and Gary Dobson were brought to trial for Stephen Lawrence's murder following the new substantial evidence: Lawrence's DNA was found on the clothes of the defendants. In January **2012**, 19 years after the racially motivated murder, Norris and Dobson were both found guilty of the murder of Stephen Lawrence and were sentenced to life. Following on from this case, in **2013,** the Prime Minister ordered an investigation into the police force due to widespread concern that police were trying to discredit the Lawrence family. This led to investigations into the procedures and tools utilised during undercover policing. It is unlikely that the other gang members who attacked Stephen will ever face charges.

1995 (US) - On the 16th of October, the Million Man March took place in Washington DC which promoted African American unity and family values.

1997 (US) - On the 25th of October, the Million Woman March was held in Philadelphia. The purpose of the march was similar to the 1995 men's march, however it instead focused on what it meant to be an African American woman.

2000 -2020

2001 (UK) - On the 16th of July, Derek Bennett, a 24-year-old father to four children, was apprehended by police following reports of a man with a gun. Bennett struggled with his mental health and doctors had recently referred him to a psychiatric ward. The 'gun' Bennett was reported to be holding was later revealed to be a novelty lighter. Bennett had held the lighter to a person's head before the man freed himself. Bennett attempted to take cover, aiming the lighter towards the police. It is then believed police shot him in the back as he tried to run away evidenced by the bullet wounds on his back. The judge declared it was a 'lawful killing.'

2003 (UK) – On the 7th of September, Michael (Mikey) Powell, who already struggled with his mental health, had a psychotic episode. Concerned for his safety, his mother called the police for assistance. The officers spoke briefly to Powell during the episode. He was then knocked down by a police car, hit with batons and violently restrained by the officers. Powell sustained serious injuries from this incident and even though the officers were aware of his mental health issues, they failed to get him medical attention. They should have taken him to a hospital but instead they took him to a police station. He died from asphyxiation due to the restraint hold he was put in whilst inside of the police van. Suggestions were made by the media that Powell was believed to have been in possession of a firearm. However, Powell did not have a gun, and they retracted the report was retracted following demands from his family for its removal.

2005 (UK) – On the 30th of April, police killed 24-year-old Azelle Rodney. Rodney had been unarmed, but the two other men in the car with him were armed. They were arrested, while Rodney was killed after police shot him six times. It is unclear why Rodney was killed. He did not have a criminal record and was only suspected of being part of an armed gang. Anthony Long, the police officer accused of murdering Azelle Rodney, claimed he thought Rodney had been reaching for a weapon when he shot him. However, Long never actually saw the weapon and there was no evidence that Rodney had one. In 2015, Anthony Long was cleared of all charges (PFOA, enquiry report).

2008 (UK) - On the 21st of August, police detained Sean Rigg after reports that he was attacking passers-by in the street. Officers arrived at the scene and restrained him for seven minutes. On arriving at the police station, Rigg was placed in a holding cell, where he collapsed and then died from cardiac arrest. Rigg had paranoid schizophrenia and had recently relapsed. This information was not relayed to other officers and the police made no attempt to look after Rigg. Nor did the mental health team did not follow the correct procedures to keep him safe. The police officers involved have been accused of lying in their statements. There is no evidence that Rigg had been violent towards members of the public when the police had been called. The level of force used was inappropriate and unsuitable for the incident. In 2014, a second inquest ruled that the original inquest was inadequate. PC Birks, one of the officers involved, attempted to resign, but his resignation was denied so that he would still face disciplinary action.

2010 (UK) - Olaseni Lewis voluntarily admitted himself into a secure hospital following the onset of mental health issues. Lewis had no history of mental illness and had been studying for a postgraduate degree. He also had no criminal record. At the hospital, within a few hours he became agitated and violent. Police were called to restrain him, however, the nurses reported being horrified by the level of restraint used. The staff said that they believed the force used by police was excessive. The cause of Lewis' death was ruled as brain stem death, but the postmortem was inconclusive in terms of whether this was a result of excessive force. In 2018, Mental Health (Use of Force) Bill, known as 'Seni's Law', received a Royal Assent from Parliament.

2011 (UK) - Kevin Clarke died from cardiac arrest after being restrained by police following concerns about his agitated behaviours. The Metropolitan Police reported that he appeared to be in 'an agitated state' when they attended the scene. Police called the paramedics before restraining Clarke so must have known he was unwell. He was taken to hospital by paramedics where he was pronounced dead. The Regional Director of the Met Police, Jonathan Green, described the police officers' actions as having breached professional standards. The use of force on people with mental health issues is unnecessary and dangerous. There needs to be adequate mental health training for police officers that is continually reviewed, refreshed, and updated according to professional medical recommendations.

2011 (UK) – On the 4th of August, in Tottenham, North London, armed officers shot Mark Duggan. The officers were acting under Operation Trident which was set up to investigate gun crime within Black communities in London. The police forced Duggan to pull over to a hard stop, following intelligence that he was suspected of being in possession of a gun and that he was planning to use it in a revenge attack for his cousin's murder. In a reconstruction based on witness statements, video footage and the police officers' statements, it was determined that Mark Duggan was shot within less than two seconds of him exiting the minicab he had been driving. Duggan was in clear sight of four officers. His left hand was in his pocket and, according to the officer who shot him, there was a gun in his right hand. However, no gun was found on Duggan, or next to him. After Mark's body had been removed for medical attention, a gun was found seven metres away from the site of the shooting. The officer who shot Mark and killed him described the gun accurately, even though would only have had the wo seconds when Duggan exited the minicab to see it. Duggan's DNA was never found on the gun and no officer witnessed the gun being thrown from the mini cab. Duggan had been shot in the arm within the first second of exiting the minicab. Medical experts also determined that it was unlikely that he could have thrown the gun with the amount of force and from the angle required to not be seen by the four officers present. It was concluded that Mark Duggan did not have a gun in his hand when police approached, therefore police's the shots were unlawful. Forensic Architecture, an independent organisation who conduct architectural techniques to assist with cases involving state violence, conducted a detailed investigation which highlighted how the various possibilities that were accepted by the IPCC were not clear cut and were contestable, and that a further option was not even investigated. The professional reports and analyses presented by Forensic Architecture are currently under review (Haroon Siddique, The Guardian Newspaper, 10th June 2020).

The killing of Mark Duggan sparked protests and riots that demanded justice for Duggan and his family. During the four days of discord, over 3,000 arrests were made and five people died. Inquest appeals have since been denied.

2011 (UK) - Kingsley Burrell was killed by the authorities that he had reach out to for help. On the

27th of March, Burrell had feared for the safety of his five-year-old son after seeing people who he believed wanted to harm him. He called the police to help to protect his son. The police arrived and called him paranoid. Burrell was then taken into custody and admitted to a mental health unit. As he was transported to the hospital, police officers attacked Burrell was attacked leaving him with lumps and swelling on his brain. His son was witness to the attack. His family were only allowed to see him once, briefly, at the hospital where they saw the extent of his injuries. Burrell was then transferred to another hospital on the 30th of March. In the ambulance, police officers restrained, beat, and threatened him. While awaiting assessment at the hospital, police again restrained Burrell using hand and leg cuffs, and left him lying face down on the floor, in a secluded room, with a blanket over his head. Medical staff had observed that his breathing was becoming dangerously slow and yet failed to act. Four and a half hours later, Burrell was found unconscious having suffered a cardiac arrest. There was a delay in providing a defibrillator and as a result, Kingsley

Burrell died from brain damage on the 31st of March. An inquest was held into the four different public services who all failed to provide Kingsley Burrell with the basic medical care, neglected him and used excessive restraint which contributed to his death.

2011 (UK) - Jacob Michael was just 25 years old when he died after police restrained him as they arrested him. Michael had called 999 to ask for help after being threatened with a gun. The police officers who responded to the call unnecessarily stormed into Michael's bedroom, where he allegedly threatened them with a hammer. The police sprayed him with pepper spray which scared him into trying to escape. Police chased Michael before apprehending him and hitting him with batons. He was restrained and put into the police van. Video footage from the cameras in the van show that Michael was in distress. He was restrained and held face down by police in a custody suite at the police station which resulted in his death. It was later stated that a history of cocaine use had also contributed to his death, alongside the actions of the police force.

2012 (US) – On the 26th of February, Trayvon Martin was shot by a Neighborhood Watch captain named George Zimmerman who is described as white Hispanic. Trayvon Martin was 17 years old and had been visiting his father in Sandford, Florida. Zimmerman had rung 911 to report a 'suspicious person' - Trayvon. Zimmerman then approached Trayvon despite being told by the 911 call handler to not to get out of his vehicle or approach the person. Zimmerman said that he shot Trayvon in self-defense and claimed that he had been injured in the confrontation. Trayvon was unarmed and had been on the phone to his girlfriend at the time of being approached. George Zimmerman was found not guilty of murder or manslaughter. On the 20th of July 2013, a week after the trial, over 100 protests and rallies were held across the US to demand justice for Trayvon Martin and call for an end to racial profiling.

2013 (UK) - Julian Cole was just 21 years old when he suffered a broken neck and brain damage after being brutally and violently restrained by police. He and his friends had been out at a nightclub when they had been asked to leave by staff. Cole had returned to the venue to ask for a refund when he was stopped by security guards who called the police. What happened in the time between the security guards and the police dragging the unconscious and handcuffed Cole with a broken and unsupported neck and spinal injury, into the police van is currently unclear. The beginning of this incident was recorded on CCTV, but not the interaction between the police officers and Cole however, there were witnesses who gave statements. The police officers in attendance later lied and claimed that Cole had spoken to them in the van and was under the influence of a considerable amount of alcohol. An ambulance was called when they arrived at the police station, and it was discovered that Cole was unresponsive. Julian Cole now has 24-hour care due to the paralysis and brain damage sustained from the incident.

2013 (UK) - On the 4th of November, police detained 39-year-old Leon Briggs under the Mental Health Act, following concerns about his behaviour. The attending officers forcefully restrained him and according to witnesses, he was visibly distressed, shouting and screaming that the handcuffs were too tight. Police took him into custody, but he was pronounced later that day when he was transferred to hospital. The officers were not charged with any offence, and nobody has been held accountable for Leon Briggs' death. This incident is yet another tragic death of a vulnerable person with mental health difficulties while in police custody.

2014 (UK) - Police were called to a party following concerns for the welfare of Adrian McDonald. McDonald had locked himself in a room and when officers arrived, he told them that he had taken drugs and was struggling to breathe.

Officers forcefully arrested McDonald and put him into a police van. He was badly bitten five times by a police dog and was tasered multiple times during the incident. McDonald began to feel paranoid and told officers again that he was struggling to breathe. No welfare checks were made by the police despite knowing that he was paranoid and distressed and that he had been injured during the arrest. McDonald repeatedly told the officers that he could not breathe, and yet they did not call an ambulance. McDonald became unconscious in the police van, but it took another nine minutes for the ambulance to be called. He was pronounced dead at the scene. Officers that had been initially charged with misconduct were cleared after the tribunal. The cause of Adrian McDonald's death was stated as drug and stress related.

2014 (US) - On the 17th of July 2014, Eric Garner was restrained in a chokehold by police officers on Staten Island, New York. Since 1993, the use of chokeholds had been banned in New York. It was alleged that Eric Garner and a friend were selling single untaxed cigarettes without a license. What started as a non-violent encounter between the police and Garner escalated rapidly into violence resulting in the death of Eric Garner. Video footage shows an officer pinning Eric face down on the ground. Garner told officers 11 times that he could not breathe during the recording. The officer's attorney claims that the officer had used a different restraint and not the illegal chokehold. Five years after the death of Eric Garner, the officer was eventually fired from the NYPD. Days before writing this, an online leak of the officer's service record, including disciplinary records, was released revealing that seven misconduct complaints had been made against him previously.

2014 (US) – On the 9th of August, in Ferguson, Missouri, Michael Brown and his friend were walking in the road when police officers stopped them and told them to use the sidewalk. The interaction escalated from a verbal exchange to violence, as an officer, Darren Wilson, fatally shot Michael Brown. Brown was unarmed and according to witnesses, his hands were raised when he was shot. Brown's death sparked protests and riots which led to the National Guard being brought in to restore order. Following the decision not to charge the officer with any crime, further protests turned violent. Five days later, the officer resigned from the police force.

In March 2015, a justice department report exposing racial bias in the justice system's treatment of Black people was released. Following the report, six employees of the police force were fired or voluntarily resigned including the then Police Chief, Thomas Jackson; the City Manager, John Shaw; a judge; a court clerk and two police officers. Later that year, two of the three seats in the council were occupied by Black people. Key roles in the community of Ferguson, which demographically has a Black majority, continue to be filled by people of colour, including the interim police chief, and the permanent replacement police chief, Delrish Moss, who was sworn in in 2016. Moss had grown up around witnessing the police's ill treatment of Black people including the death of his friend, and his own experience of being unwarrantedly stopped and searched. In a report from Emily Shapiro, Moss stated how he hope 'to diversify the police department' (ABC News, 9th May 2016).

2014 (US) - Michelle Cusseaux was a 50-year-old woman who had mental health issues. In August, under court instruction, following concerns from her mother that she needed help, Police went to her apartment. Michelle refused to answer the door and officers forced their way in. Upon entering Michelle was found holding a hammer which an officer deemed enough of a threat to fatally shoot her. Sergeant Dupra, the officer who shot her, claimed self-defense for his actions. The Phoenix Police Department decided that Dupra did not follow the correct protocol and acted in violation of policy and demoted him. Michelle's family have fought for justice, against racial inequality and for mental health to be recognised as a disability.

2015 (UK) - Sheku Bayoh was 31 when he died in police custody in Kirkcaldy, Scotland on the 3rd of May 2015. He was a dad to two young boys, one aged 3 years and the other one just 3 months. Eleven officers restrained Sheku using handcuffs and leg restraints while he was in custody. It is said that Bayoh was under the influence of the drug 'Flakka,' which can cause uncontrollable and aggressive behaviour. He had chased and assaulted one of the female officers due to the drug. Initially, the police lied to Bayoh's family about how he died, saying that he had been found in the street, before admitting that he had died in police custody. The family believes that there was a racial motivation behind his death due to asphyxiation in restraint, although the cause of death has been attributed to drug abuse.

2015 (UK) - On the 11th of December, in North London, armed police shot and killed 28-year-old Jermaine Baker. Baker had been involved in an attempt to free a prisoner from a prison van. Baker had been reaching to his shoulder where the strap of his bag was when police, believing he was reaching for a weapon, shot him. A weapon had been found in the footwell of the car, but it was concluded that Baker would have been unable to reach it. The police officer who shot Baker claimed self-defence. In August 2018, disciplinary procedures were dropped against the officer. In 2019, four years after the incident, a public inquiry was finally held, after being initially dismissed by the CPS. The officer was found to have acted lawfully as it would be reasonable to assume that Baker may have been armed due to the gangs' intentions. However, there were 24 failings found in the way the operation was planned and conducted.

2015 (US) – While being held in police custody, Natasha McKenna was tasered four times. She was naked except for a hood that had been placed over her head. McKenna had bipolar disorder and schizophrenia. She was being held there before being transferred to a psychiatric unit for treatment. McKenna had originally called police to report an assault but had ended up being arrested herself. Her death was classed as an accident and no charges have been filed.

2015 (UK) - Daniel Adewole was 16 years old when he died. He had an epileptic seizure in his cell at a youth offender institution in Cookham Wood, where he was serving a six- month detention and training order. His neurology review appointment had been cancelled days before, by the institution staff, following concerns that he and his family were aware of the appointment date – it would be against protocol for appointments to be known in advance in these circumstances. At first, the night guard on duty did not realise that Adewole was in his cell because the entry card was missing from the door, so he assumed there were just bedclothes on the floor when he looked in. After checking the files and discovering that Adewole was in the cell, the officer then went on a break with a colleague. This was just after 6am. An ambulance was called 38 minutes after the officer had discovered that he was in the cell and that he was not in his bed. The ambulance arrived and medical staff attempted to give him emergency help, but Adewole was pronounced dead at 7.44am. In the report by the clinical reviewer, it was found that the officers were not adequately knowledgeable about Daniel's epilepsy and that urgent care should have been sought far earlier.

Following Daniel Adewole's death, recommendations have been made to ensure that appointments are not cancelled for children unless health care staff have reviewed the options, or if there are sufficient security concerns. Individual care plans should include emergency cell entry protocols where necessary, and all staff should be aware of what to do in an emergency for the individual young person's condition.

2016 (UK) - Mzee Mohammed Daley was an 18-year-old man who had diagnoses of autism spectrum disorder (ASD) and attention deficit hyperactivity disorder (ADHD). He had also been diagnosed with PTSD after being attacked and stabbed by five white men, in 2014. Dakey was unsurprisingly paranoid and fearful. He had also expressed feeling harassed by the police on various occasions before his death. On the day that he died, he was acting erratically. There were alleged claims that he was seen with a knife although witnesses said that he did not seem threatening. He went into a fast-food restaurant where he climbed over the counter and was apprehended by the security staff. The police arrived and restrained him face down with his hands handcuffed behind his back. Security officers failed to inform the police that Daley was no longer in possession of a knife. Witness statements claim that when Daley was carried out into the street he was 'motionless' and that the police had not attempted any emergency first aid, nor did they seem concerned. At the hospital, Daley was pronounced dead. Key moments of care for Daley were missed, from the point of his mother contacting both the mental health crisis team, and the police service as she was concerned about him not taking his medication, right up to him being carried out to the street. His death was recorded as death by natural causes as the pathology report was inconclusive as impact of the polices' restraint.

2016 (UK) - Before Sarah Reed's death, police and other authorities that have a duty of care failed her. In 2003, her newborn baby died suddenly. The hospice where she was staying did not help with arrangements for undertakers and instead forced Sarah to take her baby herself. The trauma of this incident caused significant mental health difficulties for Reed. In 2014, she was viciously assaulted by PC Kiddie after being suspected of shoplifting. CCTV footage showed how PC Kiddie dragged Reed by her hair and punched her three times. PC Kiddie was found guilty of the assault. On the 11th of February 2016, Reed was found dead in her prison cell after having hung herself. She was on remand for an assault charge and had been waiting a medical review regarding whether she was fit to submit her plea. She was denied treatment throughout her time on remand and the judge deemed that it was brutal and cruel for someone to be denied medical care, particularly after everything she had already been through. The prison failed in their duty of care for those with mental health problems, and in the administering and monitoring prescribed medication.

2017 (UK) - Nuno Cardoso was a law student studying at Ruskin College in Oxford. On the 24th of November, he engaged in an argument that was reported to the police. The attending police officers arrested him, hit him with batons, and restrained him. He was suspected of attempting to swallow drugs. The correct procedure for this is to take the individual to hospital to be checked if they are suspected of doing so. Thames Valley police officers failed to get Cardoso medical attention. They claimed that they did not know that he had done so. However, on a video recording, the officers were heard discussing the possibility that he had swallowed drugs, and witnesses stated that he had been talking as if he had something in his mouth. Instead of taking him to the hospital a few minutes away from the college, he was taken to Abingdon Police Station. Cardoso became sweaty and slumped into his seat after seeming to bite on something. It was only then that police officers gave Cardoso first aid attention and called an ambulance. He was taken to the hospital where he died the following day.

"The police encounter a variety of people, many of whom are vulnerable, unwell, or intoxicated. Recent inquests have highlighted failures or delays in police responding to dangerous situations as medical emergencies. Too often this is based on a suspicion of people feigning illness or a problem, **particularly those from Black and minority ethnic groups."**

Deborah Coles, Director of Inquest

2017 (UK) - Edir Da Costa was one of four men to die in five weeks from being restrained by police. Police officer had selected him to do a 'Stop and Search,' At some point, Da Costa placed a packet into his mouth. Officers sprayed CS gas close to his face, hit him twice and laid him face down in the prone position with his hands handcuffed behind his back. While being restrained, Da Costa started to have difficulty breathing, however, at the time officers believed the noises he was making were yawns. He became unresponsive and an ambulance was called. The dispatch controller relayed the wrong location which caused significant delays in getting urgent medical attention to Da Costa. He was admitted to hospital and remained unconscious until his death shortly after the incident. The police failed in their duty of care by not checking on the welfare of the man they had in their custody, and in failing to recognise that Da Costa was choking and struggling to breathe. The inquest concluded that the result of death was misadventure. No charges were filed against the officers.

2017 (UK) - Rashan Charles died after being forcefully restrained by a police officer. He had been involved with the police previously. On this occasion, the officer used what is known as the 'Seatbelt Maneuver' and tackled Charles to the ground. The officer later claimed that he had suspected Charles had a weapon, but he did not offer any reasonable grounds for suspecting this, which is a key requirement for searching a person for a weapon. Before Charles had been restrained on the floor, he had put a package into his mouth. The officer claimed to have seen him put something in his mouth, yet CCTV footage does not support this. It has not been investigated as to why the officer chose to restrain Rashan on the ground rather than the standing restraint techniques. The officer asked a member of the public to assist him in restraining Charles by pinning his legs down. To alert the officer that something was wrong, Charles tapped on the door of the fridge which was inside the convenience store where he was being restrained. He then became still and unresponsive with his eyes open. The officer attempted to search his mouth for the object while shouting at him to spit it out. According to Rashan Charles' uncle, Rod Charles, a retired Chief Inspector from the Metropolitan Police, a mouth search should never be undertaken alone. The IOPC (Independent Office for Police Conduct) claimed that Charles had become unwell before the restraint, but CCTV footage shows otherwise. The police officer did not call for an ambulance, instead he called for backup. Charles remained restrained until the police medic arrived. From his own experience Rod Charles believes the force used against Rashan must have been excessive and prolonged. The force used, the dismissal of signs of distress combined with the delay in getting medical attention were all contributing factors to Rashan Charles' death. Yet the IOPC claims that the restraint used did not contribute, nor were the officer's failings deemed intentional, and therefore no charges have been made.

2017 (UK) - Darren Cumberbatch was living in a bail hostel shortly after being released from prison. Staff at the hostel had become concerned about his behaviour and they contacted the police as he seemed agitated, paranoid, and fearful. He suffered from anxiety and depression, but it is unclear whether staff were aware of this. When the police arrived, Cumberbatch locked himself in a small toilet cubicle which officers forced their way into 10 minutes later. The officers later stated that they had no plan as to what would happen when they managed to gain access. On entering the cubicle, the seven officers brutally beat Cumberbatch. According to Daniel Machover, from Hickman and Rose Solicitors, "police used considerable restraint on Darren including baton strikes other physical strikes, multiple punches, stamping, PAVA spray, Tasers and handcuffing […] the police's restraint of Darren contributed to his death." The inquest found that there were inadequate attempts at de-escalation and communication was ineffective. Officers asked the hostel staff to call for an ambulance but did not provide the full details of his symptoms or injuries. Darren was taken to hospital in a police van and was restrained on the ground with leg restraints as well. Darren continued to be restrained whilst in hospital. He died on the 19th of July as the result of organ failure, from cocaine use and the after-effects of being restrained.

2018 (US) - Botham Jean was killed by Amber Guyger, an off-duty, white police officer when she entered Jean's apartment believing it was her own. Guyger shot Jean who lived above her, as he was sitting in his living room. Concern was raised following a delay in taking Guyger to custody and the initial charge of manslaughter. The New York Times and CNN News reported that Guyger was found guilty of the murder of Jean. This was after it was discovered that she had posted racists comments on her social media accounts. In her statement, she had claimed that she feared for her life when she saw the dark silhouette on entering her apartment and that she shot Jean when he had started to walk toward to her. However, the position and direction of the bullet did not support this claim. Dallas is a diverse city. The presiding judge was Black, as were many of the jurors. It raises the question of the outcome had this been a majority white jury. Guyger was sentenced to 10 years in prison.

2018 (US) - Shali Tilson, aged 22, died in a solitary cell following his arrest during a psychotic episode. Tilson had bipolar disorder and schizophrenia. His mother had attempted to get him to seek help during this episode, but he was unable to and so had called the police to help him. On the day of his arrest, the 3rd of March, it was obvious that Shali was suffering with his mental health. Officers said it seemed like he was on drugs. Tilson was attempting to access a stranger's home, claiming to know the occupant, while shouting incoherent phrases. He refused to get out of the police vehicle when they got to the station. He was taken into the solitary cell that was easily accessible by staff and put on suicide watch. There was no sink or tap inside the cell, and so water had to be provided by the officers. Tilson was kept in his cell for nine days. During this time officers failed to check on Shali despite his constant banging on the cell door, and even when he fell quiet no checks were made as officers assumed that he was sleeping. They had failed to provide him with any water for 3 days. When a sergeant finally checked on Tilson, he was not breathing, and his skin was cold to touch.

The deputy was fired, and four other people were suspended for failing to provide basic care. The grand jury found that Shali Tilson's death was avoidable, and that lack of actions of the officers and medical staff were to blame due to assumptions, lack of training, and a refusal to follow policies. One officer falsified a statement saying that Tilson had been checked at regular intervals, yet video evidence determined that this was false. Nobody has faced criminal charges however as Tilson's death was not found to be intentional.

The Independent Office for Police Conduct 2017/18 annual statistical report identified the highest number of deaths recorded in or following police custody since 2004, 17 involving the use of force and restraint.

The following deaths happened while the victim was in contact with police officers and took place in the years 2019 to 2020.

Trevor Smith, UK, died on the 15th of March 2019 at around 5am, after being shot with in the chest with a single bullet, in the bedroom of his flat as it was searched by police with a warrant. Allegedly there was another firearm found in the building, however this has not been confirmed. On 16th of November 2021, the Coroner's Court at the inquest of the police shooting of Trevor Smith was found to be a 'lawful killing' by West Midlands police officers in attendance. (Inquest.org.uk)

Atatiana Jefferson, US, was playing video games with her nephew in her own home, on the 12th of October 2019, when a concerned neighbour called the police after noticing Jefferson's door was slightly open. Officers arrived at the property and an officer shot Jefferson as she looked out of the window to see what was happening. She was pronounced dead at the scene. In December of 2022, Aaron Dean was convicted of manslaughter. He received an 11-year and 10-month sentence and is eligible for parole once half his sentence has been served.

Breonna Taylor, US, on the **13th of March 2020**, was shot during a 'No-Knock, No-Warning' property search in her apartment in Louisville, Kentucky. It was believed that the police were investigating two men for drug charges and that packages were possibly being delivered to the apartment of Breonna Taylor. Taylor was not under investigation, and no drugs were ever found at the residence. In an act of defence, Taylor's boyfriend, Mr. Walker, shot at police with his licensed firearm, hitting an officer non-fatally in the leg. Officers returned fire and shot Taylor eight times, killing her. In his call to 911, Mr. Walker stated that somebody had kicked in the door and shot his girlfriend, who was a first responder and EMT worker. The polices' incident report had multiple inconsistencies. The officers were initially charged with attempted murder, but it was put on hold until after the inquest. In 2022, Brett Hankinson, who was charged with 'wanton endangerment' for the shots that he fired that passed through the apartment into a neighbour's home via a glass door, was found 'not guilty'. Hankinson was charged with civil rights violations for the use of excess force. Former police officers: Kelly Hanna Goodlet, Kyle Meany and Joshua Jaynes were also present and two officers who fired the shots that killed Ms. Taylor, were cleared of charges relating directly to Ms. Taylor's death. They had been investigated of falsifying the search warrant. In August 2022, Goodlet pleaded guilty to knowing about the falsified evidence and conspiring with

Joshua Jaynes to cover up the falsified information on the document. Goodlet was convicted. Jaynes and Meany were both charged with civil rights violations and obstruction of justice. The trials for them, and Hankinson, were postponed from October 2022 to the following year. 'No Knock' searches have now been banned by city officials.

George Floyd, US, was apprehended by officers on the 25th of May 2020. A young convenience store clerk reported to police that a man, who was a regular customer, (Floyd) had paid for a packet of cigarettes with a counterfeit $20 bill. 46-year-old Floyd was sitting with two other people in a vehicle near the convenience store. Two police officers approached the vehicle. One of them had already drawn his handgun and asked Floyd to show his hands. The officers pulled Floyd from the car and put him in handcuffs which he resisted. It was only after Floyd had been put in handcuffs that the officer explained that he was being detained for using counterfeit money. As they tried to take him to the police car, Floyd started to resist telling the officers that he felt claustrophobic. He did not resist violently but fell to the ground. Two more officers arrived, and all four attempted to put him into the police car. Five minutes later, one of the officers, Derek Chauvin, pulled Floyd away from the vehicle which caused him to again fall to the ground. Officers then restrained him while Chauvin had his knee on the area at the back of Floyd's head and his neck. After begging and pleading that he could not breathe, Chauvin refused to remove the knee hold – a practice not yet illegal in the state, but, like all holds, should only be used for a reasonable and just amount of time and less dangerous holds should be opted for. George Floyd died after being restrained for 8 minutes and 46 seconds. Chauvin was convicted of the murder of George Floyd and is serving 22 and a half years in prison. In July 2022, he was also charged with violation of George Floyd's rights and sentenced to a further 21 years. Local resent, John Pope Jr had told the court that he had also been subject to Chauvin's violation for his rights when he was just 14 years old, hitting him with a torch and kneeling on his neck during an arrest. Another resident: Zoya Code also filed a report against Chauvin, Chauvin also plead guilty for these crimes as part of his agreement with the prosecution.

Rayshard Brooks, US, a father to three children and stepfather to one, was killed on the **12th of June 2020** in Atlanta, by an officer who had previously covered up a shooting of another Black man. Brooks had fallen asleep in his car in a Drive-Thru Lane when officers were called. He failed a sobriety test but managed to hold calm conversation with the officers for up to 40 minutes before a scuffle ensued when the officers tried to handcuff him. Brooks had taken a taser from one of the officers, Garrett Rolfe, and ran away pointing the taser towards the officer. Rolfe shot Brooks twice in the back and then kicked him. He was heard saying 'I got him.' It took at least two minutes before Brooks received any medical attention. Garrett Rolfe had been fired from the police force and had been granted bail while facing 11 charges including a potential life imprisonment sentence of the murder of Rayshard Brooks. The other officer has been put on desk duty and is facing two charges including aggravated assault. In August 2022, all charges were dismissed against the officers as the court found that the shooting was 'justified' and that the 'use of deadly force was objectively reasonable' *(reported by Fox5 Atlanta, 23.8.22)*

" We work vigorously for freedom and justice for Black people and, by extension, all people" Black Lives Matter movement.

"I can't breathe."

"As medical students, we are taught to jump into action when we hear these words. They are universally recognized as a cry for help to which we should respond immediately and do whatever it takes to help our patients breathe again. "

LaShyra Nolen 'Med page Today' 2nd June 2020

What is Institutional Racism?

Institutional racism is defined by Oxford Languages as "racial discrimination that has become established as normal behaviour within a society or organization."

The belief that the effect of racial bias in society is reflected in policing rings true. The proportion of the Black population to white is small, yet the percentage of the Black population who have been killed due to the colour of their skin is considerably higher than the percentage of the white population if the numbers were in proportion to each other. Despite changes in the law that attempt to enforce equality, such as the Equality Act 2010, there remains instilled, problematic perceptions that Black people are dangerous, guilty of wrongdoing, assumed to be violent or aggressive, and of being more than capable of committing violent criminal acts. These preconceptions elicit extreme reactions.

The Equality and Human Rights Commission states that "if everyone has a fair chance in life, we all thrive." But while there is prejudice and racial bias not everyone will have a fair chance. Socio-economic situations that began immediately after slavery was abolished continue to contribute to a deepening imbalance in opportunity. Practices such as zoning, outpricing, and exemption from certain discounts in housing; inequal school resources and quality of education leading to lower test scores and unfair perception of intelligence; businesses moving out of areas with high Black population and removing potential work into white areas all contribute to disadvantages that perpetuate all aspects of life. Default segregation continues. Despite the implementation of laws, including the 'protected characteristics' under the Equality Act, Black people are still discriminated against by employers, estate agents, and credit agencies. Sometimes this is due to the policies surrounding those organisations. For example, housing and credit are based on employment income, homeowner status, and credit score. Typically, Black people are in lower working classes with limited job opportunities, and in lower pay brackets without any ability to obtain their own property. The same applies to accessing the required higher education to get into the higher paying middle-class roles. Employers are no longer able to discriminate based on nationality and skin colour, as well as gender, sexuality, and age. This does not mean that discrimination does not happen. People are still discriminated against, but it is under the guise of 'experience' or 'suitability.' A standard response such as 'there was somebody more suited to the role' can roughly translate as 'a Black person does not represent our company image.' But this form of discrimination is harder to prove. One comparatively legitimate response which is quite common is experience. Many people, including white people, struggle to get work without a certain amount of previous experience. However, white students are more likely to have the financial backing to allow them to take on unpaid internships and work experience opportunities which gives them an advantage when it comes to applications.

A study carried out by Marianne Bertrand and Sendhil Mullainathan looked at how responses to job applications differed depending on the name of the application. They applied to jobs using either popular African American/ethnic names or popular 'white' names. The responses showed that there was a preference for white sounding names, even if they were less experienced. Even before an interview, racial bias gets in the way.

Unsurprisingly, the same discriminative views are held in the police force and underpin the actions of law enforcement officers. These acts of discrimination are defended by the argument that police also take white lives. They are, but at a less proportionate rate than the Black population, and with less excessive force. Having wrestled with the numbers myself, I attempted to investigate this on a more manageable scale, as there is a lot of data to consider. However, there was a clear pattern. Between the 1960s and the 1980s, the majority of deaths caused by police shootings were related to the ongoing war on terrorism of the IRA. Excluding these deaths, around 42 white people were killed by the police.

Throughout this chapter we have seen stories of fast reactions, without thought for consequence. The poor judgment and excessive force of white officers toward Black individuals. Nearly all of the deaths and assaults documented here had links to mental health illnesses (some of which included substance misuse); there were unarmed suspects; low-level criminal acts which escalated into violence, delays in administering medical attention and the use of excessive, prolonged force or restraint without justified reason. These accounts of innocent Black people being murdered by law enforcement agents in their own homes without due course are unforgiveable.

In two cities in the US, white officers' weapons were fired as much as five times more than those of Black officers attending largely Black populated areas. The socio-economic situations of those areas often result in higher crime rates. Social policy should be continually changed and updated to reflect this, to bring the quality of life of Black and Minority Ethnic (BAME) people level with white people. Ensuring that 'a jury of your peers' in a court includes those who have similar life experiences to the accused particularly regarding the mitigating factors and sentencing of the case is only fair.

There is a call for a reformed police force, for more accurate and detailed data to be collected to show the levels of force used across the board and the misrepresentation to be detailed more clearly surrounding BAME deaths by armed police. There are demands for the police to be disbanded. Data submitted from police officers in the US in 2019 to the FBI regarding the use of weapons was provided from just 40% of all officers. Some areas are worse than others. It is also noted that data is not submitted centrally or internally in any systematic and nationally recognised way. It is not compulsory in all the states to record data. Real-time data cannot be used for making policies when it is incomplete and inaccurate.

The names of some other people who have lost their lives to police brutality and should be remembered, however, there are so many more and the list continues to build:

Kenneth Chamberlain, 2011 US.

Cynthia Fields, 2018 US.

Deborah Danner, 2016 US.

Christian Taylor, 2015 US.

Sam Dubose, 2015, US,

John Crawford, 2014, US.

Tanisha Anderson, 2014, US.

Nuwnah LaRoche and Jason Champion, 2015, US

Oscar Grant, 2009, US.

Aiyana Jones aged 7, 2010, US.

Kimani Gray, 2013, US.

And there will be more names. The list of those killed by law enforcement and people in positions of power will continue to increase until institutional racism is identified and addressed, microaggressions erased, and true civil rights are afforded to all. When law enforcement agencies are also bound by the law of the state and of their duty of care to all.

Chapter 5: The Abuse of Power in Trusted Positions of Authority

Armed Police

In the previous chapter we discussed how widespread institutional racism is in both the UK and the US. Throughout the chapter, there were examples of how the police repeatedly use brutality against ethnic minorities, particularly in situations related to deportation.

In this chapter, we will look at how the policies and procedures that governments put in place affect those with the least power. Using their legitimate power over the general population, as demonstrated in the power stacking table and description of a power pyramid in the introduction.

I think it important to note here before this goes to print that since the research into this book has been concluded there have been more incidents as sadly this is an ongoing concern. The latest incident to date (20th September 2023) has today resulted in charges of Murder being brought upon the police officer who fatally shot an unarmed Black man, Chris Kaba, in Streatham London, on the 5th of September 2022.

The following entries document how armed police have abused their power prior to this incident.

On the 22nd of September 1999, police officers shot and killed **Harry Stanley**. The police had been wrongly informed that Stanley was carrying a sawn-off shotgun in a plastic bag, but it was in fact a table leg. On his way home from collecting it from his brother, Stanley had stopped at a pub for a drink. Armed police arrived, and following a misunderstanding with Stanley, they shot him in the head and left hand as he turned to face them, resulting in his death.

On the 1st of April 2009, a police officer assaulted **Ian Tomlinson** during violent police clashes with G20 protesters in London. Thousands of people joined the protest which aimed to bring London to 'a standstill.' Tomlinson, a 47-year-old newspaper seller, had not been involved with the protests. As he attempted to navigate a route home, unable to avoid the cordoned-off areas, PC Simon Harwood hit Tomlinson with a police baton and pushed him to the ground. Despite getting up and continuing his journey home, minutes later he collapsed and subsequently died. A video of the incident that was published showed the attack which has been debated to be resulted in some way to Tomlinson's death. The official cause has never been determined due to disagreements between pathologists. On 3rd May 2011 Harwood was ruled as using 'excessive and unreasonable force' 'however the verdict of 'not guilty' was reached on 19th July 2012, with the defense citing Tomlinson's alcohol abuse as relevant to the cause of death. Harwood was however dismissed from service on the grounds of gross misconduct during the incident. The MPS paid an out-of-court compensation settlement to Ian Tomlinson's family in 2013.

On the 3rd of March 2012, the Greater Manchester Firearms Unit killed **Anthony Grainger.** Police believed that Grainger, and the two other people in the car with him, were going to 'hold up' a supermarket and were in possession of firearms. The officers shot Grainger in the chest as he leant forward because they thought he was reaching down to pick up a weapon. However, no firearms were found in the vehicle or on the other passengers. It is now thought that Grainger was reaching for the door handle to exit the vehicle. The commanding officers' misinformation and an inadequate operation briefing contributed to the reporting officers' fatally poor judgement. Judge Thomas Teague QC concluded in his report on 11th July 2019 that the police did not follow correct procedures, the operation had deficiencies in the planning and in the conduct, and that the inquiry had unveiled inaccuracies, institutional incompetence, dishonesty, and corruption.

The Inquiry, which began in 2013 found 16 failings within the operation that resulted in the death of Anthony Grainger. One of the failings was that the police officers who were present at the scene had the opportunity to discuss their statements and match up their version of events before their submission to the proceedings.

On the 22nd of July 2005, armed police shot and killed **Jean Charles de Menezes,** a 27-year-old Brazilian electrician, at Stockwell tube station in London.
Metropolitan Police Service were still following anti-terrorist operations following on from the four coordinated extremist terrorist attacks on public transport in London on the 7th of that month that had resulted in 52 deaths and over 750 people injured. Officers had followed De Menezes from a property they had under surveillance. The officers followed De Menezes as he travelled on a bus, then, as he boarded a train, they shot him. The Metropolitan Police claimed that De Menezes refused to follow police instructions and that his clothing and behaviour had raised concerns. These claims were later found to be false. The police gave De Menezes no warning of their intention to shoot. Officers said they thought that De Menezes looked like the 'Ethiopian Hussain Osman.' However,

photographic evidence shows that there were far more differences between their appearances than similarities. No charges were brought against the officers involved in the murder of Jean Charles De Menezes. On the 2nd of August 2007, an investigation into the conduct of the Metropolitan Police Service found that information released to the public regarding De Menezes and that claim that he was not cooperating with the officers were incorrect, nor was he wearing any clothing that could have been deemed as suspicious.

In 1994, an officer forcibly restrained and killed **Richard O'Brien**, a 37-year-old Irishman. Police had received reports that O'Brien was drunk and acting in a disorderly manner while waiting for a taxi with his wife and 14-year-old son. Both his wife and son have both disputed the claims made about O'Brien's conduct. It is believed that an officer pushed O'Brien, who retaliated. The officer then knelt on O'Brien's back for over five minutes. The police officers made racial remarks about O'Brien's Irish heritage and pulled his hair whilst they put his 'limp body into the van.' Within 10 minutes of his arrest, O'Brien had suffered extensive facial injuries and asphyxia during the restraint, thought to be resulting in his death. Amnesty International has raised concerns about unlawful killing by restraint, however, there was insufficient evidence to charge the officers involved.

On the 18th of January 2016, police shot 26-year-old **Daniel Shaver** in a hotel hallway in Mesa, Arizona, after responding to reports that a weapon was being pointed out of a hotel window. Shaver worked in pest control and, as part of his equipment, had air guns in the room with him, but no firearms were found. Shaver was intoxicated but unarmed and fully complied with the attending officers' commands. The officers' bodycam footage showed how the officers repeatedly shouted commands and directions at Shaver, who was clearly terrified and confused, before shooting him. Brailsford, one of the attending officers, was charged with but not convicted of second-degree murder.

On the 26th of December 2015, at around 4.25am, 55-year-old mother of four; **Bettie Jones** attempted to help her neighbours – The Le Griers. **Quintonio Le Grier** was a 19-year-old engineering student. Quintonio's father had called the police for help with his son's unusually distressed behaviour. He had hoped the police could help him to get medical assistance for Quintonio. It was found that prior to his father calling 911, Quintonio Le Grier had called to ask for help three times but that dispatchers are reported to have 'dismissed' the calls because he was refusing to answer their questions. Quintonio was shot 6 times, and Bettie once- she was killed "accidently". In 2019, the officer who killed Jones and Le Grier was fired but has since applied to be reinstated.

On June 16th, 2015, a police sergeant**, Philip Seidle** killed his ex-wife, **Tamara Wilson-Seidle,** with his service weapon by shooting at her through her car after crashing into it, from his own in front of their 7-year-old daughter. This was allegedly due to jealousy of Tamaras new relationship after they had been separated for over 3 years.

Prior to her murder, police had been contacted multiple times due to domestic disputes that had been violent including in 2012 when police had been called to another domestic dispute between Seidle and Tamara. This time Seidle had attempted to cancel the dispatch of officers. He was suspended for two days, and his firearm was confiscated. It was however later returned to him; this was the weapon he later used to fatally shoot Tamara. Following his arrest, Seidle's records were released, and these showed many incidents of domestic violence, some of which were sent to internal affairs to be investigated, resulting in a 682-page history. These warnings should have been acted on, and Seidle should not have had access to a firearm.

Off-Duty Armed Officers

It is important to include these incidents. If these officers had not been armed at the time - for example, if their weapons were only available to them while they were on duty or there were tighter measures on licensed personal firearms – would these deaths have happened? There is a clear pattern of off-duty officers using firearms to kill their wives, girlfriends, and even children. Off-duty officers killed the following women.

In April 2016, in New Mexico, an off-duty police officer, Mark Contreras, killed his ex-girlfriend, **Nikki Bascom**, and then killed himself.
The same month, in Albany New York, another off-duty police officer, Israel Roman, killed his wife, **Deborah Roman**, and their 10-year-old son **Nathan** with his federal-use weapon before wrapping them in blankets, setting fire to their home, and finally taking his own life.
In July 2016, an off-duty officer, Mark Elferdink of Emmett Township, shot and killed his wife, **Hope Elferdink**, with his personal weapon. He later took his own life, their 2 children 12 and 13 years old were in the home at the time.
In August 2016 in Florida, another off-duty officer, Danny Carrero was in a relationship with Mistie Reynolds and had used agency equipment to hack

into and look through his girlfriend's phone before he killed her and then killed himself.

In the same month, also in Florida, an officer killed Mary Knowlton. Knowlton, 73, had been taking part in a 'shoot/don't shoot' civilian role-playing scenario when the officer had fired at her with what was supposed to be a blank cartridge weapon. The officer accepted a second-degree manslaughter charge. The force had completed these public demonstrations for 2 years without incident as usually the firearms are either fake or unloaded. It is not clear how the firearm used for the demonstration was loaded with live rounds, but it was found that the officer, along with others, was unable to tell the difference between the fake and live ammunition cartridges.

In November 2016, in North Caroline and California, two off-duty police officers killed their wives, **Rebecka Pearce by her husband Jeremy with their 2 young children locked safely in a bedroom, and Greta Kurian was killed by her husband Kyle Kurian.** Both men then shot themselves. The incidents happened within 10 days of each other but were unrelated.

Deportation Officers and Policies

Asylum Seekers leave their homes to escape war, natural disasters, gang, or drug-related violence, and political or persecution reasons, they flee to countries outside of the area of conflict requesting refugee status. During World War I, children in England were evacuated from the cities to the countryside to escape bombing. They were removed from a place deemed too dangerous and relocated. Why are international refugee children treated with indifference if they too are removing themselves from a dangerous place to a safer one? The act of deportation all too often serves as an unlawful death sentence. For example, people come to the US from Mexico, undocumented, to raise their families in safety, work hard, and do no harm. All the while living in fear that the decisions of a handful of people in positions of power could mean deportation. Deportation breaks up families. When children are separated from their parents this can lead to mental health difficulties, struggles with identity, and incite fear and loathing of the country that separated them. People are deported back to countries where they could be killed on sight because of gang or drug-related violence. Women attempting to escape domestic violence through seeking refuge face the possibility of being returned to the person trying to harm them. Interestingly, in 1942, after the US had joined World War II, a ship of refugees coming to the US unknowingly brought over Herbert Karl Friedrich Bahr, a German spy who was posing as a refugee. He was born in Germany but had obtained American citizenship after moving there as a child. In 1938, while working in Germany as an engineer Nazi officials approached him to spy for them. During his trial, Bahr claimed that he had planned to reveal everything to the US Government but was scared that other German spies would find out. This fueled paranoia throughout the US. **Attorney General Francis Biddle advised President Roosevelt** to refuse immigrant status to new arrivals. Further restrictions were introduced and refugees from Germany and Austria were denied entry to the US. President Roosevelt believed that there were Jewish people who had been coerced into spying for the Nazis trying to enter the country. This unfounded fear continues to underpin immigration policies in the US today.

The following examples show how foreign nationals have died because procedures were followed incorrectly during deportations.

In 1993, Joy Gardener was unlawfully killed when the UK Home Office ordered her and her five-year old's son deportation back to Jamaica. Following an investigation, Amnesty International released a report on the incident which revealed that the Home Office had not followed the correct procedures. They had purposefully delayed sending the letters which would have informed Gardner that her application to remain in the UK had been denied. They also refused to allow Gardener to speak with her solicitor during an unannounced deportation visit to her home. In addition, statements taken by officers, who had gagged and restrained Gardener, were full of discrepancies. In 1995, the Crown Prosecution Service charged three officers from the Alien

Deportation Group with manslaughter, but they were all acquitted.

On the 12th of October 2011, Jimmy Mubenga, a father of five, died in the custody of G4S - a security firm contracted for arranging deportations. Mubenga was pronounced dead after being restrained on a plane at Heathrow Airport as he was due to be deported to Angola. Before takeoff, crew members and other passengers reported that Mubenga had repeatedly cried out and pleaded that he could not breathe. G4S have consistently failed to train their staff appropriately, and in some cases, they have not provided the necessary training on how to safely restrain deportees. Guards and staff from the firm reported that they have expressed concerns to their superiors, including insufficient training, poorly controlled guards, and the risk to detainee lives. G4S have consistently failed to provide the services they are contracted for, and yet, they continue to be employed. It is unclear why a company which fails to meet contractual terms continues to keep those contracts and does not appear to take responsibility or financial action to rectify its mistakes.

In 2011, the UK Government introduced policies that required employers and doctors to verify citizenship through identity documents. Authorities had not provided the Windrush generation from after World War II with any legal documentation on their arrival in the UK, so they were unable to prove their 'citizenship' under these new policies. They were denied access to employment, education, medical services, and travel, and then were detained and deported. The victims of the Windrush scandal and their families continue to struggle and fight against these policies.

> *"See, people with power understand exactly one thing: violence."*
> Noam Chomsky

Pharmaceutical Companies

Pharmaceutical companies have expert power. They are trusted to conduct risk assessments, ensure the safety of medicine, and highlight risks to those who take it. The manufacture and distribution of thalidomide in the 1950s is a clear example of the misuse of expert power.

In 1956, a Chemie Grünenthal employee gave birth to the first baby affected by the drug, Thalidomide. It was a drug given to expectant mothers in the 1950s. The original manufacturers of the drug, Chemie Grünenthal, began dispensing it to pregnant mothers as a sedative to help with sleep and morning sickness symptoms. At the time, doctors believed that morning sickness was a psychosomatic symptom, and that if mothers were overexcited about their pregnancy, it could trigger symptoms. It was thought that a sedative would help to calm the expectant mother down and subside any sickness.

Thalidomide had the expected result of relieving morning sickness. According to one expectant mother at the time, some doctors called it a 'miracle drug.' However, the expectant mothers who had taken the drug gave birth to babies with severe deformities, which affected their extremities such as their legs, arms, and ears. The drug attacked the baby's nervous system while they were in the womb, causing the defects.

In the UK, Distillers manufactured and prescribed thalidomide under the name 'distal' between 1954 and 1961. In 1961, William McBride, an Australian doctor, announced the formal link between thalidomide and birth defects. Despite claiming they were unaware that the drug would cross the placenta barrier, Chemie Grünenthal was the first to withdraw it from manufacturing on the 26th of November, and on the 2nd of December, Distillers followed suit.

Doctors told the expectant mothers who had taken thalidomide that their babies were unlikely to survive. There were several incidences where doctors and nurses took the newborn babies and killed them in 'mercy killings,' either by suffocating them or by leaving them on a metal slab in a cold room immediately after birth. In 2011, *The Independent* reported that Dr. Richard Nicholson, the editor of the Bulletin of Medical Ethics, had admitted to taking part in 'mercy killings' as a junior doctor 20 years ago *(The Independent,* October 2011*)*.

In February 1968, the 62 families affected by thalidomide in the UK finally won their case against the manufacturers. The UK Government had deemed the case too weak, leaving the families to seek justice independently. In Germany, the trial against Chemie Grünenthal for involuntary manslaughter and intent to commit bodily harm was closed in 1970 because it was deemed to no longer in the public's interest to continue the case.

Under the statute of limitations law, (a time limit in which cases need to be filed within a court to be heard), it would be deemed that 369 other families affected by thalidomide were too late to bring their case to court however the statute time limit was lifted for these cases. Initially, Distillers offered these families a settlement that was half the amount given to the original 62 families, and it was on the grounds that all the families had to accept it or none of them would receive it. Five families refused the offer, and the court took custody of their children. During the legal proceedings, a parent of a child affected by thalidomide approached *The Daily Mail* to print an article exposing the failings of the manufacturers and the courts. After releasing the article, *The Daily Mail* was found in contempt of court. Distillers continued to apply for injunctions and claimed further contempt of court as the media attempted to release articles that exposed the original findings and paperwork from the German manufacturers.

> *"An exception to the confidentiality rule might be if disclosure documents reveal acts of such iniquity that publication would be justified in the public interest. The response was protection of discovery documents was more important."*

(Phillip Knightley (1997), *The Independent,* 24 August)

In 1973, after further information had been released, Distillers agreed a final settlement. In 2012, the German manufacturers issued a formal apology to the survivors. Many felt that they should have offered ongoing financial assistance to the victims still struggling with the repercussions of the drug.

Around 10,000 babies born were affected by the drug, and less than 3,000 of those affected are still alive today. In the UK, there are reportedly 452 families who have been affected. The survivors face ongoing pain, tingling, numbness, loss of strength, mobility problems and other health conditions. Their lives must be adapted, and they often require ongoing assistance for everyday tasks. Many thalidomide survivors have had children of their own. Their deformities have not been passed on which means the drug did not affect their genetic makeup.

Today, thalidomide is used in various medications and treatment processes for certain types of cancers and other illnesses. However, restrictions are in place, particularly for women, due to the now widely known risks of birth defects. Interestingly, Nazi chemists and scientists who worked under the supervision of Nazi Doctor, Josef Mengele in World War II, were later recruited by Chemie Grünenthal and other pharmaceutical companies across the globe, including Otto Ambros. Compounds of thalidomide are thought to have been used during WWII in Nazi laboratories.

Chapter 6: Issues of Power and Misrepresentation in The Media

Owen Jones, a columnist for *The Guardian* and author of 'The Establishment and How They Get Away With It,' is a renowned critic of mainstream media and a whistleblower for 'right–wing biases within mainstream media. In an article from 2019, titled 'Why We Need to Talk About the Media's Role in Far-Right Radicalisation' Jones argues that "Much of the British Press incites hatred against minorities" (Jones, Owen (2019), *The Guardian*, 28 March). His argument is supported by The Independent Press Standards Organisation's (IPSO) request that *The Daily Express* and *The Sun,* both UK-based newspapers, be held accountable for irresponsible journalism. The IPSO demanded that the newspapers make statements acknowledging that the claims they had made in reference to unsubstantiated statistics about the Muslim community in Britain were misleading and that they dangerously misrepresented British Muslims.

In 2017, the website You Gov conducted a research poll about the newspapers publicly perceived political stances. The results indicated that *The Daily Mail* was believed to be the 'most right-wing' newspaper in the UK. *The Guardian* was considered to be the 'most left–wing' and *The Independent* was thought to be the most central, as its name suggests, independent of political bias.

Journalists were once responsible for obtaining facts and delivering the news as they discovered it. Now they are being provided with more scripted versions of the news to present to the general public. In his book, 'Flat Earth News,' Nick Davies describes how news content has been produced with the 'systemic omission' of facts as political forces drive and shape news stories to solely benefit those already in power. He explains that journalism's 'neutrality' has been replaced with opinion and propaganda to intentionally provoke a reaction from the general population.

In 'Folk Devils and Moral Panics,' Stanley Cohen writes about how the media portrays deviancy from societal norms and how information is then structured and processed in a way that fits the political landscape. Cohen explains that the information that journalists and media presenters receive is 'second hand;' it has been filtered and altered to suit a political objective. Cohen observes that the media often uses vague language and poses thought provoking questions to the public. The public then takes the time to think about what they have heard, feeling as though they are in control of what they are thinking, in a world where control is hard to come by. The ideas given that what has been reported is not acceptable within society and reinforcing those social normative behaviours and expectations.

Noam Chomsky likens America's 'campaigns of public diplomacy' to propaganda. In his essay entitled "Prerogatives of Power" in his book 'Because We Say So,' Chomsky explains that news is made favorable to those in positions of unchallenged power. The process of what Chomsky terms "historical engineering" and the ability to ignore 'unwanted facts' only serves as tools to serve the needs of those in power.

Media Control

Malcolm X was vocal about how the media is a 'powerful entity' and can control how and what the public thinks. He described how newspapers can dictate public opinion and tell them to like or dislike certain groups. He also warned this control can be changed quickly. In one interview Malcolm X spoke about how throughout World War II American people were made to believe that Russia and China were their allies, but Germany and Japan were the enemy states. Yet this political climate quickly changed and therefore so did the minds of the people.

In 'Manufacturing Consent,' Edward Herman and Noam Chomsky set out a 'propaganda model.' They explain that news coverage goes through 'five filters' before being presented as being non-biased and objective. Herman and Chomsky believe that the media is owned and monopolised by the wealthy and powerful through adverts. Their theory is subject to the idea that those in bureaucratic positions are credible and trustworthy because of their positions in society. The content, therefore, has the inability to change from the narrative due to fear of going against assumed public consensus and ultimately losing viewers, readers, and revenue from advertisers. Finally, that they encourage and assist in creating a common enemy, a common goal which unites the people.

War Propaganda

During World War II, both sides used propaganda for assorted reasons, but ultimately to gain support.

One well-known example is a poster which included the phrase 'loose lips might sink ships' that would have been displayed prominently near amenities that women would use such as grocers, doctors' offices, etc. This was a warning to the women to not talk too much because enemy spies might overhear. But what if the posters were not just about supporting the war effort, demonizing the enemy, and encouraging people to play their part? What if those posters in particular stopped people talking about the war effort, to avoid the possibility of a debate about the war or the politics behind it? Posters, broadcasts, and strict rules incited fear in the public about the consequences of talking too much. One poster in the United States, for example, showed an image of a woman who allegedly had been carelessly speaking about the war effort, and as a result of such action people had died, the fictional woman portrayed was then accused of murder.

Both sides used emotive language and images to invoke feelings of sadness, disgust, fear, and patriotism. They were intentional in creating a sense of paranoia about who could be trusted and who might be dangerous, from neighbours to friends, colleagues, and strangers. The public was encouraged to be wary of one another, creating a general atmosphere of distrust. The only people who could be trusted were the Government. Printed material that portrayed fingers pointing, people dying, and eyes watching were displayed in every shop, workplace, and street to keep these ideas in people's brains. The 'blackout' rules were displayed in public. They were useful when needed but otherwise created fear. The colours of a country's flags were often used in propaganda to remind people of the duty to their country. Parents were encouraged to send their children out of cities to the countryside through propaganda which warned of the harm their children may come to otherwise. One poster, shown at the Imperial War Museum in London, depicts a mother thinking of sending her children to a place of safety, with an image of Hitler above her telling her not to, to warn that the enemy wants to keep children in harm's way.

Nazi propaganda often featured depictions of Jewish people who were blamed for the war. One example consisted of the British, American, and Russian flags, with a Jewish man hiding behind the Iron Curtain, insinuating that Jews were controlling the enemy.

One poster that was taken out of distribution was an image of Adolf Hitler, smartly dressed, with the slogan 'Adolf Hitler is Victory.' However, after the

Stalingrad defeat, it was no longer deemed appropriate to distribute these.

Allied countries would air drop printed materials with fake news or send out radio messages that appeared to be real, but in fact were false.

Political Smear Campaigns and Misdirection

Smear campaigns are used to misinform, redirect, and spread doubt about someone (or something) through published events, broadcasts, and reports. They are an attempt to discredit someone by making false allegations. They tend to be political and occur mostly around elections, as opposite sides will attempt to find out anything that could demonise or show the other side as untrustworthy to the voters in an attempt to win. As smear campaigns are typically published, the media should be held responsible for fact checking reports before they are printed. IPSO can regulate it, but only after it has been published, by which time the damage may have been done.

In the 'Academic Report of Journalistic Representations of Jeremy Corbyn,' directed by Dr.

Bart Cammaerts, the team investigate and review the journalism surrounding the rise of Jeremy Corbyn within the Labour Party and his campaign to become Prime Minister. The report shows that many newspapers were antagonistic towards Jeremy Corbyn in their reporting, some far more than others, like *The Daily Express* and *The Sun*. Corbyn was delegitimized by the media which likely swayed a number of people to change their minds about voting for him and the Labour Party. The report demonstrates how the media villainized Corbyn to excess and with aggression that misrepresented him and damaged his political reputation. The media repeatedly took what he said out of context in order to portray him as an unsatisfactory opposition to the Conservative Party. The study uncovered some interesting statistics regarding the platform Corbyn was given by the media. It was revealed that in over 50% of the articles examined, Corbyn's words, statements and opinions had not been included. It was also noted that a substantial proportion of his views expressed were taken out of context. Ultimately, the media was providing a false and negative portrayal of the Labour Party's leader and the main opposition to Boris Johnson. Table 3 in their report shows how the majority of media content was scornful or mocking towards Corbyn. In *The Daily Express,* 80% of the coverage was considered to be 'ridicule and scorn'. 40% of overall coverage of Corbyn was a 'personal attack'. This level of antagonizing, sensationalizing, singling out and villainizing of a public figure is not very productive nor unbiased. In fact, it is undemocratic.

If we look at the recent US presidential campaigns, Donald Trump consistently accused Joe Biden of lying, cheating and fraud. He did the same with Hilary Clinton before. In June 2016, Trump made a comment about Clinton being a private person, saying that nobody knows anything about her religious views. This was an attempt to discredit her as he was speaking with Christian leaders. In August 2016, Trump made an unprovoked remark that Barack Obama and "crooked" Hilary Clinton founded ISIS. Trump had previously said that the Obama administration was actively supporting Al

Qaeda. He also claimed that Hilary Clinton was going to release all the violent criminal from prisons. These comments were unfounded and untrue. Throughout his presidency, Trump randomly claimed that there were so many terrorist attacks that they were going unreported. His seemingly racist and misogynist views spread like wildfire. He spouted statistics that were incorrect and made off - hand comments. His comments were broadcast, printed and distributed. Those who followed President Trump, or those unsure of who to vote for, were being manipulated, not just by these comments, but also by feeling the need to keep the status quo and the norm. Statements and statistics that fuel hatred, scaremonger, and feed off the insecurities of the general population, so much so, that is forced into the subconsciousness by way of microaggressions, covert racism, smear campaigns, lack of or altered context, misrepresentations, and stereotyping that is forced through the media.

Social Media

New mass media platforms, the rise in misinformation and incitement of hatred have caused a number of issues. Political voices rallying via online social media platforms such as Twitter, to gain attention, support, and inciting violence, for example the Trump supporters storming the Capitol Building after attending a Trump rally and listening to a speech made by Trump, repeated and replayed via social media, that the New York Times reported as "riddled with violent imagery and calls to fight harder than before" (Savage, C. (2021), New York Times Online, 10 January)

Social media platform creators should take responsibility for limiting comments to prevent the spread of speculation, assumptions, racism, and hatred. There also needs to be full support from governments. The security, guidelines and policies of social media are considerably flawed. They provide platforms where everyone can contribute. However, while this can be a good thing, it can also be bad. Hate, lies, misunderstandings, scorn, and mockery can be distributed freely. Social media is a vast, uncontrollable, and mainly uncensored machine. A narcissist's haven, where poison spills and gossip grows under fake accounts, run by untraceable and anonymous people. What is put out into the online world never goes away, lies cannot be easily retracted nor corrected like in newspapers or news reporting. Sharing damaging images, comments, and lies has never been easier. We call for uncensored controlled media to ensure that democracy can be true, yet uncensored misinformation can be shared in non-controlled media formats. This is the wrong way around. Books and news are able, if the need arises, to provide evidence, and ask for sources of their information so that facts can be told. Social media is full of opinions based on hearsay and the sharing of wrong or misleading information.

Misrepresentation of Groups of People and the Use of Stereotyping.

Stereotypes are everywhere. Stereotyping takes a group of people and claims that they are all the same because of one or more of the following: lifestyle, beliefs, language, culture, religion, or intellect. They are often cruel and demeaning. Stereotypes are harmful yet they are still a huge part of our ignorant society. Television programs, books, songs, films, plays, magazines, and cartoons can all influence how we see groups of people. Some take on forms of generalisation, like how all women are the 'same.' The media plays a crucial role in building a picture of how other people live, and promoting the social conventions people are expected to adhere to.

When news stations are reporting on a crime, the offender's skin colour is often taken into consideration, if they are not white. But why? You do not tend to hear that 'a White man with blue eyes has been charged with manslaughter.' When the police are searching for a suspect then skin colour is relevant to identify a person. One's skin colour, religion, culture, birthplace, sexuality, gender, disability, or age are helpful to know – however if the media is going to distinguish between a white person and a Black person, it needs to be done both ways. Legally protected characteristics should not be used as descriptors when reporting on a fact to prevent the demonization of groups of people. What help is it to describe a person's characteristics? Especially with the technology we have today, photographic images can tell us enough about a person. Due to the differences of power, advantage, status and socio-economic situations, there will likely be similarities among offenders, but due to these issues or their individual characters, not their skin colour or sexuality.

Misrepresentation within Films and TV Programs.

People have long been misrepresented based on their social status. Single mothers are often shown to be from rundown local authority estates in urban areas, cigarettes hanging out of their mouths with a vast array of children following or in buggies along with cans of Coke and crisps. This can lead to comments on social media from ignorant people who claim that all single mothers are on benefits, and that the dads are all MIA or 'deadbeats.' This may be the case for some single mums, but there are plenty of other single parents out there who do not fit this stereotype, but they get caught up in these generalisations and are assumed to be this way. Likewise, if you are a single parent but have a high-flying career and a great support network people assume that there are no children, or that the dad helps out., again, this is not always the case. In film and TV, middle class families are typically represented as the perfect nuclear family, 2, opposite gender parents with two children and perhaps a well-behaved pet, living in an immaculately presented home, the epitome of the 'desired' family life.

In film, Black actors have historically played roles where they are seen as negative members of society from crooks to robbers, drug dealers, rapists, murderers…the list goes on. Over time, Black people were portrayed more like White people, ignoring the various and educating cultures of Black people, and miseducating society on what Black people "should" be like. Seeing any other way as antisocial or non-conforming and therefore negative. There is still a lack of representation in the film industry. Some films feature White people with painted Black faces playing a Black person's role, blackface, which is extremely offensive.

Cartoons directed at adults, but often accessed by easily influenced adolescents, use a variety of stereotypes, misrepresentations, and negative depictions to create 'humour' for their audiences. However, the content being used, again, reinforces those stereotypes in real life. Stereotypes are damaging. They impact how people are seen. Equality laws are in force, but equality laws do not change opinions.

Magazines select women that fit the beauty standards. They airbrush and edit images, creating a false image of reality. Men are also chosen for their appearance. The more this goes on, it creates a stereotype of what people should look like. They are nothing but adverts designed to make people want the products sold, in the hope that if they buy it, the outfit will automatically suit them and change their body shape, the console makes someone look as 'cool' as that dude, the bag makes someone look wealthier than they are. They are misrepresentations of real life. The trend of selfies on social media with filters designed to make a person change their appearance to fit into the figure of beauty they saw on the front page of that glossy magazine. Gay men are often portrayed as one type of person, loud and colourful and in love with glittery and 'girly' things. Some people are like that because they want to be, but some are not. Either way, one person's existence does not count for a group of people.

The War on 'Terrorism'

Hatred toward Muslim people has been more prevalent since the 9/11 attacks. On the 9th of September 2001, two passenger aircraft purposefully flew into the North and South towers of the World Trade Centre in the US. This was reported across the world. People in the towers, aboard the planes and the emergency crews who tried to help those injured and trapped were needlessly killed. The event was shocking, tragic and horrifying to watch or read about, let alone be there.

In his book, 'Stupid White Men' Michael Moore compared George Orwell's book '1984' to how society is with politicians, and the connection is quite real. "The leader needed to have a 'permanent war.' He needed to keep the citizens in perpetual fear of the enemy so they would give him all the power he desired' (Moore, M, p.260). Moore goes on to say that politicians make people fearful that the "enemy [is] everywhere, anywhere, and that they could die at any moment" so they can detract from the real issues that society has, giving a common enemy to focus on, rather than focusing on what the democratic society has been reduced to.

In his book 'America's Addiction to Terrorism,' Henry Giroux writes about similar themes and goes into far more detail on this particular area of interest. Giroux compares the physical acts of interrogation of suspected 'terrorists' under the Bush administration to the acts of violence the 'war on terrorism' is trying to prevent. He also likens the treatment to other cases of human rights violations. Giroux shares statistics that reveal that a considerable proportion of America's citizens believe that the physical torture of other human beings is justified, in these circumstances, as it would prevent further acts of terror. This proportion of American people believe that human rights can be sacrificed where someone in power deems it to be necessary.

The Afghanistan War built public support using media platforms. George W Bush and Tony Blair, the UK Prime Minister in 2011, publicly advocated for the war on Iraq and Afghanistan in retaliation to the 9/11 attack. However, as discussed in the previous chapter, it is argued that the UK and US's invasion was illegal. The media used images of pro-war activists in their reports of the war. The front page of *Lawrence Journal-World* on Thursday 20th of March 2003 was segmented into different reports about the start of the war. At the bottom of the page, it showed a photograph of a young woman holding up a sign which says 'Be a Real American, Support Troops' suggesting that if you do not support the war effort, then you are not a true citizen. There is no photograph on the page that represents the alternative side to that argument.

The media was openly enraged at Blair for his apology for the Iraqi war in 2015. *The Daily Mirror* overtly opposed the war, actively printing anti-war material, and supporting anti-war protests. But it was the majority of the media that encouraged the population of the UK to support the war. The media consistently reported that the war was an end to the vast number of weapons of mass destruction being produced under Saddam Hussein's regime. These allegations were later found to be false. On the 5th of July 2016, *The Conversation* reported that media representatives claimed they had printed what they had been told to, without checking the information, they had received this information from someone in a position of authority. This type of reporting is dangerous. The general population can only go by what they have been told or shown by the media. If media platforms are publishing false stories, misleading, and misdirecting the public then this is abuse of power. It violates human rights, democracy, and freedom of thought. Can the media be trusted as a non-biased source of information? No.

Chapter 7: Hate Crimes against the Muslim Community

In this chapter, we will look at the experience of Muslim communities in Western countries, focusing on the acts of terrorism committed by White Western people towards Muslims. Exploring the works of Henry Giroux, Doug Sanders and other theorists, this chapter sets out the basic premises of Western extremist ideology. We will explore the ideology that fuels such hatred. In 'America's Addiction to Terrorism,' Henry Giroux writes about his views on terrorism in America. However, this addiction is not just an American problem.

Here I will give a brief overview of an answer to the question 'When did the divide between Islam and the West begin?'

How the Islamic Empire was established.

There were clashes between the Hashim and the Quraysh tribes until 630AC when the Quraysh people allowed Muslims to control the city of Mecca. The Prophet Muhammed (the founder of Islam) died and despite there being no named successor, Abu Bakr became the first of 'The Four Rightly Guided' Caliphs. During his leadership, Bakr invaded the Byzantine Empire. In 634, he was succeeded by Omar (Umar), the second Caliph, who had been born into the Hashim tribe. Umar conquered Jerusalem, Damascus, Babylon, Egypt, and Persia. Umar was murdered by a Persian slave, and Uthman became the third Caliph. He successfully conquered Alexandria, Armenia, Africa, Cyprus, and Rhodes. He was assassinated and replaced by the fourth 'Rightly Guided Caliph,' Ali, in 656. The Battle of the Camel was fought that same year between Uthman and the rebel group run by Aisha, a widow of the Prophet Muhammed, and his relatives and companions who wanted to overthrow Uthman as they believed that he was guilty of corruption and nepotism. Ali had opposed the violence and rejected the rebels' request for a leader. The rebels marched on Basra. During pre-battle negotiations, Aisha called for Ali to be removed and an election to be held. Ali refused and he gave clear instructions that wounded, unarmed, and captured fighters from the opposing camp would not be killed. The battle took place in the December of 656. The battle ended when Aisha's camel was killed, and she was captured. Aisha was treated well and was returned to Mecca (Medina) to continue to live in her home as Muhammed's widow, where she had been expected to stay following the Prophet's death.

Ali freed prisoners and allowed them to be pardoned for their parts, including high ranking members of the rebel party. Ali was assassinated with the use of poison, coated over a sword, in 661.

Christians also occupied parts of the Middle East, including Baghdad.

In 1099, Christian crusaders, under the orders of the Pope, captured Jerusalem and ended the Empire. The conflict between the religions continued for seven crusades, spanning 151 years, and finally ended in 1250. However, religious difference was only one part of the conflict. Land ownership – such as the ongoing Israel-Palestine conflict – power, politics and imperialism were other contributing factors.

Some historians argue that these were more important than religion.

The West continues to be involved in the East. For example, Jerusalem is still a key area of conflict. It is a specified Holy land for three religions: Islam, Christianity, and Judaism. The Israel-Palestinian conflict was, in summary, due to the potential division of Jerusalem. The USA continues to provide arms and financial aid to Israel. Part of Palestine was gifted to the Jewish community after World War II when it was under British rule. The battle for land and power continues as both sides believe they have the most right to the land, including access to Jerusalem.

Counter-Terrorism Policies and the Indoctrination of Fear

The 'War on Terror' was coined by US President George Bush in 2001. 'America's Addiction to Terrorism' was written by Giroux in response to the 9/11 attack on the World Trade Centre, and the ongoing use of fear, by governments, to control the masses. Giroux argues that the increase in security and the disregard for liberty and democratic values has turned the United States into a fearful country; paranoia is indirectly encouraged through fearmongering and increased police intervention. After the 9/11 attack and then the attack on the Pentagon in 2001, the US advanced their surveillance and security to 'nanny state'. Deep nationalist feelings and the need for retaliation were heightened. The mainstream media spread propaganda and warmongering advanced, inciting fears that terrorists were poisoning water and food supplies. By heightening security, it fueled a desire among civilians for further violence.

Having the power to decide what constitutes terrorism can be abused.
In 2011, the Prime Minister David Cameron, with the Conservative Government, set up The Prevent Agenda, a program delivered to those who work with children to train how to identify potential extremism behaviours and language'. It was expanded in 2013, following the murder of Fusilier Lee Rigby. The

Prevent Agenda is part of an attempt to combat terrorism, aiming to identify individuals vulnerable to radicalisation by extremist groups and prevent their indoctrination. Under the strategy, support is given to individuals considered vulnerable and at risk. 'British values' - democracy, law, liberty, and respect for different beliefs and faiths – are promoted. However, it is difficult to monitor as individuals will have different motivations for their extremism and ways of acting on it.

In the UK, the right to freedom of speech and expression is limited. Hate speech and content that is considered potentially harmful to the public is prohibited.

In 2019, the UK Government criticised Hackney council for failing to make any referrals to an agency set up to help in preventing radicalisation. In a council meeting, reported by the 'Hackney Citizen,' Tracey Thomas, the council officer in charge of coordination of preventative anti-terrorism measures, argued that Hackney is a less vulnerable area than other neighbouring boroughs (Sheridan, E. 18th July 2019).

The Prevent Agenda is designed to safeguard young people and educate them on their views in an open and age-appropriate way. A wide-held criticism of counter-terrorism strategies is that it is not clear how the programs identify and safeguard people against 'White nationalism and extremism' when White terrorists are typically extremely nationalistic and abuse the ideas of British values. 'British values' can be a disguise for more extremist, typically racist views, making it difficult to gather evidence or prosecute individuals. In this sense, the Prevent Agenda is covertly discriminative of institutional racism due to being more open of international related extremism over domestic extremist views. There are human rights lawyers, teachers, and others from the Muslim community who disagree with the Prevent Agenda strategy. They argue that it is counter-productive and discriminates against some of the protected characteristics of people, such as those from Muslim backgrounds. Henry Giroux shares the same thinking in his book 'America's Addiction to Terrorism.' Giroux argues that America's counter-terrorism strategy and the 'War on Terror' also known as the GWOT -the Global War on terrorism "mimics the very crimes it pledged to eliminate" (Giroux, 2016). In the book, he discusses the lies told by President George W. Bush and government officials to the American public about Iraq to justify new anti-terrorism laws and strategies including the torture of suspected terrorists. Bush abused the power that he and the Government held to declare a 'National State of Emergency.' In the UK, Prime Minister Tony Blair supported President Bush in his war on terrorism, and his systematic and counter-effective approach. The Chilcot Inquiry report, published in 2016, concluded that it was unnecessary to invade Iraq and that Bush had not followed the UN Security Council's advice. General Abdul Wahed Shannan Al Rabbat, the former Army Chief of Staff in Iraq, attempted to prosecute Tony Blair for his 'crime of aggression' in related to the Iraq War. However, the High Court rejected the bid for prosecution as a 'crime of aggression' is not recognised as a criminal offence under UK law.

Since the extremist terrorist group Al-Qaeda attacked the World Trade centre on 9/11, xenophobia and Islamophobia have increased significantly. They have become a prominent feature in everyday life. It has highlighted this issue and spread fear to wider audiences, particularly with the advance in technology, internet use and social media. This has turned into a witch hunt against Muslim people, making them out to be folk devils- representations of people to be scared of, with ongoing and unfounded suspicion of anyone who follows Islam. The Bush/Blair conflict in Afghanistan has further exasperated Islamophobia and the fear of Muslim extremism.

At the centre of Islamophobia, seems to be the fear that the Muslim community will become the majority, leading to the eventual extinction of White Christian people. Organisations like Britain First (a political group who claim to want to put the needs of British people first, and who use this ideal to harass and demonise the Muslim community in Britain) push the belief that Muslim people are attempting to introduce Sharia laws and the Islamic faith in Britain, to replace Christianity in the Western world.

Examples of generalised criticisms of the Muslim community are usually about their supposed 'refusal to assimilate to Western culture.' There is a consensus that 'if they don't like our ways, they should go back to their own country.' Abusive comments can often be heard about the physical appearance, cultural dress, skin colour, or public acts of faith such as prayer, dietary requirements, and the customs of the Muslim community. It appears to be the belief that those with Islamic culture should leave it behind if they wish to live in the UK.

Religious faith in the West has decreased over the past century. But religion is still used to excuse behaviour. Secularisation is more common in the West but as a society, we hold onto the history of being a deeply religious country where the Christian Bible was followed and believed.

Many Westerners believe that the Qur'an is filled with extremist views that encourage terrorism. But the Bible and other holy books are also filled with so called violence and illegal customs. The laws and customs of a nation are widely based on the religion of the country or in the case of Britain – the Sovereign– and therefore laws that are based on Islamic faith are rejected by Western countries. Sharia councils that were formally recognised within the UK in 1996 have caused uproar as they accommodate the cultural customs of Islamic law within the West.

In Doug Sanders' book 'The Myth of the Muslim-Tide,' he explores the West's historical distrust of other religions and cultures, especially Catholicism and Judaism. The Islamic community is the latest group of people to experience the wrath of Western extremist views and close-mindedness. The widespread Islamophobia we see today is comparable to the prejudiced beliefs of the KKK, the Nazis and other white supremacist groups.

Xenophobic Crimes and Terrorist Acts against Muslims

One widely known terrorist is Anders Breivik. In 2011, in Norway, Breivik published a document stating his hatred for Muslims and his fears of an Islamic takeover. He had been influenced by other countries' increasingly strict immigration policies. Breivik bombed a government building in Oslo, intending to punish and kill the politicians he viewed as 'traitors.' Breivik then travelled to the island of Utoya where the Labour Party Youth summer camp was being held. He proceeded to shoot and kill 69 people, including children. He wanted to stop them from being 'tolerant' of the Muslim community. Breivik believed in 'Eurabia' (far right, anti-muslim mindset) and the alleged possibility of the destruction of Europe's cultures and customs as Islam replaces them. This is a common theme in Western extremist views and can be viewed as the main cause of the ongoing conflict, growing terrorism, retaliation, and hatred toward the Muslim community in Western countries.

In June 2004, three 14-year-old youths attacked Yasir Abdelmouttalib, a 22-year-old student.

Abdelmouttalib was on his way to Finsbury Park Mosque in London and was wearing traditional robes for prayer. The three youths began to verbally abuse Abdelmouttalib and spit at him as he boarded the bus. As he got off the bus, they followed him and at least one of the youths attacked Abdelmouttalib with a road sweeper's broom, as well as punching and kicking him. The attack left Adbelmouttalib paralyzed, partially blind and with serious brain damage. On the 29th of November 2004, Harrow court acquitted two of the youths of all charges. The other youth was sentenced for causing grievous bodily harm with intent.

In this incident, the police pursued an incredibly detailed avenue of inquiry into Yasir Adbelmouttalib's - the victim's - motives, actions, and clothes. This is a clear case of victim-blaming. Officials also kept a remarkably close eye on Adbelmouttalib while he received treatment for his injuries. They claimed this was because of his residency status. If Adbelmouttalib was not Muslim, nor in traditional clothing, nor in a society where the 'War on Terror' was so prominent, would the police enquiries have followed the same victim-blaming line?

On the 10th of August 2007, 43-year-old Brian Donegan attacked and blinded Sheikh Mohamed Al Salamouny, the Imam at London's Regents Park Mosque. The location of the attack and the identity of the victim may suggest potential Islamophobia, however Donegal has since been detained under the Mental Health Act indefinitely and, as a result, was found not guilty on the charges. I feel that this case should be included as it is quite clear why there was a lack of media attention despite the horrific injuries the victim sustained, the fact that there was an Islami element.

In July 2005, a gang attacked Kamal Raza Butt, a 48-year-old man, who was visiting his family in Nottingham. The incident took place outside a corner shop at around 4:30pm. The gang shouted 'Taliban' at Butt before beating him. Butt died in hospital from his injuries. Two youths were charged, one received an 18-month detention and training order, a specific order granted to youths in youth court that specifies how a convicted of a crime could be rehabilitated (trained). Charges were dropped against the second youth as witnesses, who had originally claimed to have seen him punch Butt in the head, refused to give evidence in court.

In 2009, in London, Neil Levington was arrested, after authorities discovered his plans for a series of attacks. Levington was inspired by the nail bomber David Copeland who had targeted Black, Asian, and gay people in a series of attacks in London in 1999. Although Levington took inspiration from Copeland, his intended targets were Muslims. The European Muslim Research Centre released a publication that accused the mainstream media of not highlighting the significance of this case. They said this was because Levington is White. The publication also mentions other incidences that have not received the same media attention as Islamic extremists. They include Martyn Gilleard who was a neo-Nazi jailed for 16 years after a raid on his home for child pornography also uncovered bombs and racist material. Robert Cottage had been a candidate for the British National Party. He believed in the need for a future civil war due to 'uncontrolled immigration' and had stockpiled chemicals and other materials to make ammunition and bombs. These were discovered after his wife called the police.

In November 2009, in Islington, London, a gang of Black and White youths attacked Muslim students at City University. They intended to 'get those Muslims,' who they believed to be terrorists. The gang made a series of attacks over several days. They stabbed, threw bricks and rocks, and hit students with weapons. They attacked Muslims as they left prayer rooms and, on their ways, home. Witnesses reported that there was minimal police presence or involvement, which allowed the attacks to continue. Police who were called to the scene were often unaware of the previous attacks and did not treat them as seriously as they might have done otherwise.

In 2009, attacks were made on The Greenwich Islamic Centre in London. The perpetrators set fire to the doors of the centre causing thousands of pounds worth of damage and injuring the caretaker who attempted to stop the fire. That same year, in May, letters of hatred were sent to the Islamic Centre in Luton before it was targeted by arsonists. There has been no reported link between the two centers, but it is thought it could be in response to the picket line of Muslims who were demonstrating against the conflict in the East as British troops returned. On Boxing Day 2009, the Cradley Heath Mosque and Education Centre was targeted. When it was rebuilt, the Mosque was laden with racist graffiti. The arson was the second time it had been attacked this way.

In a report credited by the *Muslim News Online*, dated Friday 16th December 2022, it was stated that almost half of the mosques and Islamic centers in the UK have experienced some sort of attack, which is religiously motivated, in the last three years. The report detailed that 17% of people worshipping in mosques in the UK have experienced physically abusive interactions with racially motivated individuals.

On the 29th of April 2013, in Small Heath, Birmingham, Pavlo Lapshyn stabbed and killed 82-year-old Mohammed Saleem as he left the Mosque after prayers. In October, Lapshyn admitted to the murder and also to planting explosives in three different areas of the West Midlands near mosques between May and July. The device he had planted in Tipton exploded on the 12th of July and Lapshyn was arrested five days later. Lapshyn was sentenced to 40 years in prison. He had told officers that he hated 'non-Whites.' Police discovered his plans for the attacks and other evidence of his white supremacist views at his home.

In November of 2015, on a subway in Toronto, two men and a woman verbally abused two Muslim women with derogatory comments such as 'go back to where you came from' and calling them 'terrorists'. The suspects took off when another passenger pressed the emergency alarm on the train. From attacks such as these the hashtag

#illridewithyou became widespread on social media to help Muslim people in Toronto to feel safer when travelling on public transport.

In 2016, in Brooklyn, New York, Emijeta Xhelili assaulted two Muslim women and their children. Xhelili kicked, hit, verbally abused the women, pulled off their Hijabs and attempted to push over their toddlers' pushchairs. Xhelili was sentenced to six months in prison for assault as a hate crime.

Also in 2016, in Brooklyn, New York, Christopher Nelson verbally abused a Muslim woman, Aml Elsokary, an off-duty police officer, and her 16-year-old son. He shouted at them to 'go back to their country' and threatened to slit their throats.

In 2016, at Grand Central Station in New York, Soha Salama was pushed down the stairs and called a terrorist as she made her way to work in her uniform and hijab. She was left with bruises and a twisted ankle. At this time, hate crime rates had spiked in New York city according to the NYPD officials, doubling from the previous year following Donald Trump's election win.

On the 29th of January 2017, Alexandre Bissonnette entered the Quebec Islamic Cultural Centre and shot and killed six people and seriously injured five others. Bissonnette claimed that he did not have Islamophobic motivations. The judge ruled that he had prejudiced intentions and sentenced him to two consecutive life sentences. In May 2022, The Supreme Court of Canada declared that Bissonette will be able to apply for parole after just 25 years. Life sentences are part of a criminal code provision which means that those who commit multiple murders are not eligible for parole for at least 50 years. However, the High Court ruled that this is degrading and violates the Charter of Rights and Freedoms guaranteed against treatment that is unusual or cruel by removing the possibility of being released before life expectancy age.

In June 2017, in Finsbury Park, London, Darren Osborne drove a hire van into a crowd of Muslims who were stood outside of a mosque. Osborne was charged with the murder of Makram Ali and the attempted murder of nine others who were injured in the attack. Osborne had recently written that he believes that Muslims are rapists, and this is believed to be due to a documentary he had recently watched, fueling his belief that Muslim men were out to rape white girls.

On 23rd of June 2017, Marek Zakrocki, a Britain First supporter, drove at and ran over Kamal Ahmed, outside the Indian takeaway establishment that Ahmed owned. Earlier that day, Zakrocki had said that he was going to kill a Muslim to his family. His daughter called the police and when they contacted him via his wife's mobile, he declared that he was 'doing it for Britain.' He made a Nazi salute and shouted "white power" before he drove his van at Ahmed. Zakrocki was sentenced to 33 weeks in prison for dangerous driving, driving under the influence and battery of his wife. However, he served those weeks on remand, and therefore walked free having spent that time out of the custodial system with his bail conditions. Zakrocki's alcoholism was said to be a factor in the sentencing decision along with a time of 'heightened tensions.' Zakrocki has been accused of other racially aggravated offences, and an attempted murder but these allegations have not been pursued. Other cases against him include a prior conviction of assault of a police officer, possession of a knife in a public place and an attempt to cause grievous bodily harm.

In Dundalk, US, a 17-year-old girl threw eggs at the house of a family who had fled from Iraq. She was charged with the destruction of property. This was the latest incidence of harassment the family had experienced. Muslim civil rights groups have since called for the police to make better attempts to protect them.

On 23rd of May 2018, in the early hours of the morning, outside of a McDonalds in St Augustine, Florida, 60-year-old John Jay Smith, armed with a knife and stun gun, approached a group of international Muslim-Egyptian students as they attempted to get into their car. Smith tried to use stun gun on the men by putting his arm into their vehicle. The driver tried to back the vehicle away but was blocked by an obstacle. It is said that Smith committed the act due to the victims' ethnic or religious backgrounds and because Smith had allegedly had a son who had been killed in the Afghanistan war. Smith had been drinking alcohol prior to the attack. The victims reported that the attack has left them shaken, struggling to sleep and unable leave the house.

In 2019, 36-year-old white supremacist David Parnham was jailed for 12 years for sending hundreds of letters inciting hatred and violence against Muslims between 2016 and 2018. The letters contained a white powder that appeared to be anthrax or a similarly toxic substance. He also sent undisclosed letters to the Prime Minister and the Royal family, as well as to the white supremacist Dylann Roof. Throughout 2017, Parnham sent letters to mosques containing death threats and threatening and violent drawings. He signed the letters 'From the Muslim Slayer.'

On 15th of March 2019, 29-year-old Brenton Tarrant live-streamed a massacre on Facebook. Tarrant attacked the Al Noor Mosque and the Linwood

Islamic Centre in Christchurch, New Zealand. He killed 51 people including a 3-year-old child and injured another 49 people. Tarrant was motivated by Islamophobia and white supremacist beliefs which he shared on social media. Prior to the attack, he had researched the layouts of the buildings to ensure maximum casualties. Tarrant owned six assault weapons, had described himself as a terrorist, and had planned for further attacks.

Within a few hours of those attacks in New Zealand, in the UK a group of White men in their 20s drove past the East London Mosque and shouted abuse out of the windows. One of the men got out of the vehicle armed with weapons and approached a 27-year-old man outside the mosque. The Muslim man was beaten with a hammer and a police-style baton while the other men from the vehicle shouted Islamophobic abuse.

In March 2020, in Edmonton, Canada, Richard Bradley Steven approached two women who were wearing hijabs. Steven shattered a window of their car and began chasing one of the women before pushing her to the ground. He then pushed the other woman to the ground as she tried to help. Stevens was charged with two counts of assault and one count of mischief.

34-year-old William von Neutegem had caught the attention of the authorities after sharing white supremacist views on social media. Von Neutegem is the main suspect for the stabbing of Mohamed-Aslim Zafi, a 58-year-old, who volunteered at a mosque in Toronto's West End. The attack happened on the 12th of September 2020. Von Neutegem has been arrested and charged with first-degree murder. He was later diagnosed with Schizophrenia and was declared as not 'not criminally responsible.'

On the 3rd of February 2021in Edmonton London, Shane Edward-Tremblay verbally threatened two Muslim women. Tremblay was being verbally and physically abusive towards a 19-year-old Muslim woman. When another woman tried to step in and defend her against Tremblay. Half an hour later Tremblay pushed one of the women and verbally threatened her. In July 2021, Tremblay was sentenced to 210 days in jail for his hate-motivated crimes.

On the 6th of June 2021, in London, Ontario, 20-year-old Nathaniel Veltman drove into the Afzaal family, killing the parents and grandparents and seriously injuring their 9-year-old child. Veltman has been charged with murdering four members of the family. Police say it was premeditated and the Muslim family were specifically targeted for their religion. Veltman was wearing swastikas and body armor when he was arrested. A witness said that he laughed afterwards. Veltman's trial is set to be held in September 2023 and is facing four counts of murder and one for attempted murder.

On the 20th of August 2020, Dean Morrice, a former UKIP member, was arrested and charged with ten counts of terrorism offences. Avon and Somerset Police released a press statement that Morrice had been sentenced for 23 years. On the 14th of June 2021, *The Guardian* reported that 18 of those years were to be spent in prison. Morrice is a neo-Nazi. He was influenced by the 2019 Christchurch Mosque shootings. Police found him in possession of the instructions on how to 3D print a handgun, as well as terrorism manuals and video footage of the mosque shootings edited to include him playing the guitar. Morrice confessed to having far right and neo-Nazi views. He said he glorified other white supremacists and crimes against 'non-Whites' and Jewish people. Although Morrice had not carried out a physical terrorist act, he had actively promoted terrorism and neo-Nazi ideology online as well as having collected materials that show an intention to commit a violent act.

On Tuesday 4th of May 2021, worshippers were hit with stones and eggs from a passing car outside of Ilford Islamic Centre in London. The attack took place at around 11pm after prayers had finished. To this date, no arrests have been made.

Paul Golding is the current leader of the far-right political party Britain First. He was previously a British National Party (BNP) district councillor. Britain First was originally set up by Jim Dowson, who also has links to the BNP. Golding and Jayda Fransen, the former deputy. Golding and the Britain First party used the murder of Lee Rigby in 2013 and the radicalisation of his extremist killers to fuel their political campaign. In 2014, they organised 'Christian patrols' which became a regular occurrence around London. The patrols attended mosques, holding banners to attract media attention, and distributed Bibles and leaflets. They would enter mosques and confront attendees about alleged Islamic grooming gangs. It was at this time that Jim Dowson left the party. Britain First members claimed that they were arrested for these patrols, and that the police were preventing them from protesting and were biased against British people.

On the 7th of March 2018, Paul Golding was fined for harassment and before that in 2016 for wearing a 'political uniform' — namely a fleece with a logo representing Britain First - clothing that affiliated him with the political party. He has served time in prison for ignoring court orders warning him against entering mosques unlawfully and encouraging others to do so. Britain First had a prominent social media presence until pressure was put on the platforms to monitor their content more closely. In 2018, Britain First was banned from Facebook for inciting racial hatred. In January 2019, Jayda Fransen, the former deputy, left the party after being imprisoned for religiously aggravated harassment.

The English Defence League (EDL) was co-founded in 2009 by Tommy Robinson (real name Stephen Christopher Yaxley-Lenonn) and Kevin Caroll. It was set up before BNP and shares similar anti-Muslim principles and aims. The EDL posits that Muslim extremism is a danger to British society. EDL members share strong beliefs that violence against women and terrorism is within Islamic texts. In 2013, Robinson and Caroll left the group, claiming that they did not agree with the growing far-right extremism within the group. This reason is highly contested by sceptics. Robinson has faced allegations of being paid by the anti-extremism group Quilliam to leave the EDL. He was sent to prison for contempt of court and has been banned from social media platforms for inciting hatred. EDL pages on social media have also been suspended, as well as their PayPal accounts.

Due to the 'dangerous organisation' status of these groups, members of the BNP, EDL and Britain First have been banned from social media. In 2016, National Action was proscribed as a terrorist organisation by Amber Rudd, the then Home Secretary, as was National Front. National Action, founded in 2013, was being monitored by the Government's Prevent program at the time. Its co-founders, Ben Raymond, and Alex Davies were both sentenced to eight years in prison for being members of a proscribed organization alongside Jack Renshaw who plotted to murder a Labour MP.

Why there are concerns from the Muslim community in relation to reporting hate crimes.

It is incredibly difficult to research the full extent of attacks on Muslim people. The media fails to report many of these incidents with the same level of attention and detail as they give to terrorist attacks and crimes carried out by Muslim extremists.

Institutionalised prejudice and bias in Western governments and other authorities make it difficult for Muslim people to report crimes. There is the fear of not being believed or not being treated with the same seriousness as crimes against White people. Crimes such as spitting, verbal abuse including threats of harm and death, pushing, and ripping off Hijabs, are often unreported by the victims. These are key microaggressions that happen frequently towards the Muslim community and can result in fatal attacks.

White supremacist and anti-Muslim rhetoric are rife throughout Western cultures. It is everyone's responsibility to call out and stop these acts of hatred, the damaging stereotypes, the media's biased reporting. It is important that we provide accurate education surrounding hate crimes to make young people aware of the impacts, morally and legally.

Chapter 8: White Terror Influence Groups

Neo-Nazis, Modern day Hitler Ideologists and White Supremacy

White supremacist groups across the globe have adopted Nazi policies and values into their own thinking, referring to it as 'patriotism.' Writing for *The Independent*, Maya Oppenheim reported that 22 million Americans surveyed believe that neo-Nazi and white supremacist views are acceptable (Oppenheim, *The Independent*, 2017). The following are white supremacist groups that share those types of views.

The National Socialist Movement (NSM) is the largest and most active neo-Nazi group in America. They accept members from other neo-Nazi and white supremacist groups as well as members with no previous associations. In 2009, it had 61 chapters throughout America. According to the Southern Poverty Law Centre, the NSM has a youth group - like the Hitler Youth - as well as divisions for women and 'skinheads.' The movement has adopted, and idolizes, Nazi ideology and policy, from using the Swastika as their emblem to holding book burnings and having a military style uniform that is worn for protests, marches, and riots. They have protested homosexuality, immigration, and Barack Obama's presidency. Notably, they demonstrated against the opening of a Holocaust Museum, attempting to intimidate and target Jewish people. One member, Ted Junker, a member of the Nazi party during World War II, attempted to open a shrine to Adolf Hitler in Wisconsin.

In April 2018, in a video interview, reporter Christopher Mathias asked Jeff Schoep, the commander of the NSM, about the use of Nazi salutes. Schoep answered that they are 'Roman salutes' not Nazi salutes - an interesting attempt at rebranding. According to *The New York Times*, Schoep is reported to have turned his back on the neo-Nazi movement following the Charlottesville rally. Many believe that his reformation is an attempt to avoid harsher punishment for his involvement in the rally which erupted into violence and led to the death of 32-year-old Heather Heyer after a car drove into crowds that were protesting against the neo-Nazi rally.

The Hundred Handers is an international reaching group active in the UK, US, Canada, Italy, and Spain. Their name is inspired by creatures from Greek mythology. In April 2020, TRT World Online profiled the group and their unique approach to stickering in public areas. During the COVID-19 pandemic, their stickers specifically blamed the spread of the virus on immigration. Other stickers have been found promoting their racist and anti-Semitic agendas such as stickers that reject Kosher and Halal foods. In April 2020, the BBC reported that arrests were made in relation to the group under racially aggravated public disorder offences.

In 'The Racist Mind: Portraits of American Neo-Nazis and Klansmen,' Raphael S. Ezekiel provides first-hand accounts of the neo-Nazis and Klansmen that he met in Detroit, in the US. Ezekiel met with the leader of the Death's-Head Strike Group, a man named Paul, after a brief telephone conversation to discuss Ezekiel's research. Paul made it clear that although Ezekiel being Jewish was not important to him, other members of the group would be suspicious. Ezekiel attended rallies and events with neo-Nazi groups, enduring stares, and remarks from many of the attendees who were deeply antisemitic. Paul told Ezekiel that he had a problem with racial integration and inter-racial relationships as he believed they would lead to the erasure of White people (p.177). Later in the book, Ezekiel recounts a meeting with another member of the Death's-Head Strike Group who expressed uncertainty about his purpose and the aims of the group. He disclosed that he struggled to understand why White people are considered to be superior and how Jewish people are trying to take over the world as Paul believed.

In another interview, a neo-Nazi group member called Raymond described how he had attacked a Jewish man with a pole. He spoke proudly of the injuries the man sustained and the repercussions of this attack. He said that if they (likeminded people and groups) had the power to, then they would send Jewish people to Israel. Raymond also told Ezekiel that if a White woman had interracial relations, then she would 'get a bullet in the brain' (p.249). Later, Ezekiel recounts how Raymond believes that Black people are 'uneducated' and therefore not as much of a threat as Jewish people are. Raymond's grandfather was an overt Holocaust denier, and this has influenced Raymond's anti-Semitic views. His grandfather would show him propaganda and cartoons, which depicted child-abusing Jewish doctors, devious looking Jewish kidnappers and accounts of Jewish child killing rituals. Raymond expressed shocking views towards people like Ezekiel's grandchildren. Ezekiel's accounts of these individuals and their beliefs are both fascinating and upsetting to read. On pages 255-256 Raymond was speaking with Ezekiel one evening about their baby who was due to be born, Ezekiel suggested that if the baby were a girl she might 'marry a Jew" Raymond responded with. 'If she does, if she marries a Jew, there'll be a rope in her future' about his own child. The conversation turned darker but in a casualized manner. Context regarding Raymond is needed from the book itself to understand the concept of how this man's brain functioned. Raymond knew that Ezekiel was a Jewish man and believed that he was a good guy. When Ezekiel suggested that perhaps his daughter might meet one of his grandchildren when they are older and fall in love. Raymond at first said that it would not happen because the plan to have removed the Jewish people should have been done in the 20 years' time frame they were thinking about. Ezekiel offered another point, that perhaps their child would meet one of his grandchildren while travelling to a future Jewish settlement and Raymond replied that if they had a son, he imagined that he would be polite enough, but in the back of his head "dreaming of a little oven."

National Action (NA) was a highly secretive group which prohibits its members from speaking out about it. On the 12th of December 2016, the UK Government classed it as a terrorist organisation and subsequently banned it. According to the Hope Not Hate organisation, Despite the prohibition of the organisation, NA members in East London were still found to be training younger people in Legion Camps – where methods of fighting, self-defense and martial arts combined with far-right ideology were combined educative tools. NA used the murder of the MP Jo Cox to encourage further terrorist acts, and honored her killer, Thomas Mair, on their social media account. The Home Secretary, Amber Rudd, condemned the group, stating that any association or support for the group would be classed as a criminal offence. National Action continue to hold anti-Semitic, racist, and homophobic public protests and demonstrations. On the 9th of June 2020, four people were jailed for being former and current members of the terrorist group. *The Guardian* reported that Alice Cutter, one of the four jailed, had competed in a 'Miss Hitler Beauty Pageant,' calling herself 'Miss Buchenwald.'

In 2015, an active neo-Nazi group named Atomwaffen Division (AWD) was founded in Texas, in the US. The AWD believe that the modern world cannot be repaired, must be destroyed through violence, and extreme depravity to create a new white supremacist world. The group holds training events, 'meetups,' where they share propaganda and teach attendees how to manage weapons. The AWD take direction and inspiration from The Order, a violent white supremacist accelerationist group that was active in the 1980s. They have implemented The Order's values into their own promotion of 'National Socialism' (Nazism – political far right ideology and practices that align with Hitler's Nazi Germany) The AWD focuses on physical meet ups and activism, and specifically state that members must be willing to be involved in acts of violence, disorder, and terrorism.

The Iron March was an online forum where neo-Nazi and white supremacist groups, such as the AWD, could meet, share ideas, and organise rallies and events of their own. It was removed from the internet in November 2017, but members have set up other forums and groups to continue to recruit people, targeting younger, more vulnerable, and impressionable individuals. Recruitment tactics also include posting flyers and stickers on university campuses which urge people to join these openly Nazi groups.

The Order of Nine Angles (ONA or O9A) began in England in the 1960s. It was founded on Nazism, fascism, satanism, and Aryanism. Members are encouraged to take the more extreme and violent ideology of the ONA to other fascist and white supremacist groups that they join. The ONA and similar groups promote acts of barbarity including the murder of babies, sexual assault, and rape. They also idolize Charles Manson, a dangerous cult leader from the 1960s and 1970s who orchestrated several murders. The more extreme ideas of some groups are a source of conflict among the collective. However, they agree on committing terrorist acts against their enemies and share an appreciation of Nazi practice. They are known for performing Nazi salutes, wearing death masks and swastikas, as well as sharing heavily influential propaganda in videos, pictures, and written articles.

As with other terrorist cells, neo-Nazi groups are secretive. They are tightly affiliated with other groups, and it is difficult to pinpoint members before they move onto new groups. However, when founders and leading members are caught then groups tend to disband quickly and regenerate elsewhere. Once a group's forums and meetups are infiltrated, charges will be brought against them by the authorities.

In February 2020, following the disbandment of National Action, the Sonnenkrieg Division, and the System Resistance Network were formed. They were also later uncovered and documented as terrorist cells making them illegal.

Neo-Nazi related propaganda and messages have been found on the anonymous and encrypted messaging app Telegram, while videos inciting violence and hatred have been discovered on the video site Bit Chute. Links to websites that encourage antisemitism, conspiracy theories and ideologies have also been found on these sites.

"I think we should make honest people out of the Jews.

If they want a Jewish holocaust written in the history books, let's give them one"!

Direct quote from f**kthejews.com

(An example of how current neo-Nazi groups express hatred among web-based forums.)

Anti-Semitic hate crime and terrorism on the rise

The classification of religious targeting as a hate crime was only introduced in 2017.

On the 27th of October 2018, in the US, Robert D. Bowers committed a neo-Nazi terrorist act. Bowers entered the Tree of Life Synagogue in Pittsburgh, Pennsylvania during the Sabbath services. He shouted, "all Jews must die" and open-fired at the worshippers. Bowers killed eleven congregants and injured six other people, including four police officers. Bowers, armed with several guns, eventually surrendered to officers whilst claiming that "Jews were committing genocide against his people."

Following this deadly attack, anti-Semitic incidents have risen across the US, from graffiti depicting hate symbols, vandalism, the desecration of Jewish cemeteries, to bomb threats to Jewish buildings, such as community centres. The Anti-Defamation League (ADL) reported that from the 1st of January until the 20th of February 2017 there were four series of anti-Semitic bomb threats across multiple states in the US. Incidents like Pittsburgh synagogue shooting have led to Jewish congregants practicing safety drills. The ADL have created a security manual to be shared through Jewish institutions to protect people from these threats and attacks, not dissimilar to those created for schools in the wake of school shootings.

In 2019, 19-year-old John Earnest entered the Chabad of Poway synagogue in California during Saturday worship. Shouting anti-Semitic slurs, he shot at the congregation. He murdered one woman as she tended to her dead mother and attempted to kill three more including the Rabbi who tried to reason with him (Cowan, J. *The New York Times*, 2019). In March 2020, it was reported that the

District Attorney of California was seeking the death penalty for Earnest. In June 2020, action was taken against those involved in supplying Earnest with the firearm that he used, including the gun shop and the manufacturer, Smith, and Wesson.

On the 30th of August 2019, Scottie Andrew for CNN news reported that there had been at least eight anti-Semitic attacks in the city of Brooklyn over a week. The NYPD also reported that between January and September of that year, there were at least 166 anti-Semitic incidents.

The ADL reports that anti-Semitic attacks increased by 12% from 2018 to 2019 in the US. There was also a 56% increase in physical assaults on Jewish people. In 2019, there were 411 antisemitic incidents reported in K-12 (Kindergarten to 12th Grade). Over half of the hate crime attacks in New York in the last year were attacks on Jewish people, with Orthodox Jews being particularly vulnerable to being targeted.

On the 27th of January 2020, the BBC reported that the UK's Community Security Trust had recorded 892 anti-Semitic incidents in the UK in the first six months of 2019. It showed an increase of 672 from the previous year. France and Germany also recorded increases in anti-Semitic attacks in 2018.

These incidents are not limited to adults, these numbers also include children. This is a reminder that children are vulnerable to being influenced by their community, family, friends, and social media which can contribute to the rise of anti-Semitic extremism.

The Holocaust has become part of history lessons all over the world but the lack of education and minimal mainstream media attention to other incidents against the Jewish community creates a focus on this one hateful historical event. There is a failure to adequately address and educate on the perhaps more low-level acts of hatred and behaviours in an attempt to prevent greater acts of violence for example shootings, attacks and the overall perception of antisemitism that exists today. Holocaust denial questions the historical accuracy of the events of the Holocaust and discredits the Jewish community and survivors, as well as fueling anti-Semitic beliefs.

Denial comes in many different forms. From the outright denial of the aims of the camps, the existence of specific death camps or methods used, to 'revisionism' which approach can be used to refute facts as exaggerated, inaccurate, or debatable.

Holocaust Denial Cases and The Struggle Against Antisemitism

Earlier in the book, while looking at the chapter surrounding War Crimes, we briefly looked at why Holocaust denial is used. Here we look further as to what this means.

The following countries have specific laws prohibiting antisemitism, including the promotion of Nazism, Holocaust denial and the use of Nazi symbolism: Austria, Belgium, the Czech Republic, Germany, France, Lithuania, Liechtenstein, Poland, Romania, the Netherlands, Slovakia, Switzerland, Spain, and Israel. Some of these countries are extremely strict with their laws. For example, Germany has made Holocaust denial illegal as it is 'an insult to personal honour.' In other countries the punishment is dependent on the incident.

The UK, Ireland, and Nordic countries have no specific laws against neo-Nazism or Holocaust denial due to their more lenient free speech policies. Antisemitism, neo-Nazism and Holocaust denial are against the law if they are part of another crime – such as hate speech, hate crimes, assault, or harassment.

Mein Kampf, Adolf Hitler's autobiographical manifesto, is banned in most European countries, including Germany and countries that were previously occupied by the Nazis.

The use of the internet, and using external, non-limited, countries to host anti-Semitic sites, to promote neo-Nazi material, music and holocaust denial remains an easily accessible avenue for young people to access antisemitic propaganda and to then share these dangerous ideologies.

Influencers of Nazi ideology and those who flout the law surrounding Holocaust denial are beginning to be penalised. In Germany, incitement to hatred, including Holocaust denial, is now a criminal offence. 16 European countries, Israel, and Canada have also adopted similar laws, with other countries implementing the persecution of Nazi ideology into their hate crime policies and legislation. The following cases are a few of these convictions to show who, where and the crime of which they were convicted.

In France, **Jean-Marie Le Pen,** a politician, and the president of the National Front, heavily promoted anti-immigration policies. He was found guilty of Holocaust denial due to his comments made in 1987 that tried to 'downplay' the Holocaust. Le Pen continued to be unconcerned with the law surrounding Holocaust denial and repeated his earlier comments and also then defended the leader of the French Nazi collaborationist Vichy regime from the 1940s who had aided the German authorities in deporting 78,000 Jewish people from France to death camps. These acts caused him to be forced out of the

National Front in 2015 and he received a £24,000 fine. Prior to this he had been convicted of contesting crimes against humanity regarding the belief of the inhumane Nazi occupation of World War II. He has also been fined for provoking hatred and ethnic discrimination in 2016.

Richard Verrel was the deputy chairman of the National Front and a known supporter of eugenics. Verrel would write about his thoughts on holocaust denial in the Spearhead Magazine of the National Front. He wrote a Holocaust denial pamphlet entitled 'Did Six Million Really Die?' which was published by the German-born Canadian Ernst Zundel. In Canada 1985, a court trial found the 'pamphlet' to be composed of misinterpretation, fabrication and misquotes. The publisher, who was also known for similar charges, was found guilty of publishing whilst knowing of its falseness and that it would lead to disruption on social and racial tolerance. Zundel would continue to incite holocaust denial. This was only recently removed from sale off Amazon in 2017.

Ursula Haverbeck, a 91-year-old Holocaust Denier, was recently convicted and sentenced to two years in prison for continuously denying the Holocaust and claiming that Auschwitz was a 'work' camp, and not a death camp. In 2016, Haverbeck denied the holocaust at an event in Berlin, she was then sentenced to six months imprisonment. Haverbeck had already been given sentences for various other holocaust denial charges. She has distributed holocaust denial pamphlets to the public, including to a judge, prosecutors, and reporters. Haverbeck has appealed her sentences in 2017 and 2020, but the court in Berlin sentenced the woman to 12 months in prison in April 2022, her sentence could not be suspended and was rejected due to the fact that she showed no remorse in court. Haverbeck has served at least 30 months for her crimes over an extended period of time and has been ordered to pay many fines also.

Horst Mahler was a lawyer in the 1960s who later co-founded the Red Army Faction, a left-wing terror group where he participated in robberies and kidnappings. During his time in prison for these crimes his extremist views turned to the right wing whilst in prison and Mahler joined Germany's far-right National Democratic Party in 2000. In 2009, he was sentenced to 10 years imprisonment on charges of Holocaust denial and incitement of racial hatred. In 2015, Mahler was temporarily released on medical grounds, but spent a lot of time at neo-Nazi rallies addressing the members and reiterating his denial of the Holocaust before attempting to evade returning to prison fleeing to Hungary, however he was extradited and was returned to complete his sentence. Now aged 84, Mahler is facing another sentence following his release for further counts of Holocaust denial and incitement of hatred of concerning online content.

In July 2019, **Karl Munter,** a former SS soldier, was arrested and charged for Holocaust denial and for claiming that the victims should be blamed for their own deaths. He was partly responsible for the killing of 86 people in Asqu, Northern France in April 1944 where he held the post of Junior Squad leader at aged

21. However, for several reasons including being unable to locate him, he was not legally prosecuted for his involvement. Munter had ties to various neo-Nazi groups. Munter died before his incitement charge was brought to trial.

In 1989, Austrian authorities issued a warrant for **David Irving's** arrest for his trivialization of the Holocaust. In 1992, Irving was fined and banned from entering Germany for denying the existence of gas chambers. He was also prohibited from entering Australia for the same reasons. In 1994, Irving spent 10 days in Pentonville prison for contempt of court. He attempted to sue Deborah Lipstadt and Penguin Books for libel in 2000. In her book, Lipstadt had claimed that Irving was a Holocaust denier, and that he supported Nazi ideology. It was a high-profile case, which cost Irving $5 million in legal fees. The judge concluded that Irving was a pro-Nazi, antisemite who had manipulated historical evidence. The trial was a victory for the living relatives of Holocaust survivors. In 2004, he was denied entry to New Zealand for Holocaust denial. He was jailed in

2005 under warrant in Austria for denying the gas chambers existence in 1989. He was then deported back to the UK.

Irving is known for authoring several books which tell World War II from the German perspective. He claims that Hitler had not known about the Holocaust (inadvertently admitting then that the Holocaust happened and then later retracting the view). Irving has long-standing connections with the National Alliance and had been known to use derogatory terms for Jewish people. In January 2017, *The Independent* reported that Irving had claimed that many of Trump's young supporters had been contacting him and agreeing with his Holocaust denial theories.

> *"I'm going to form an association of Auschwitz Survivors, Survivors of the Holocaust and Other Liars...or the ASSHOLs."*
>
> David Irving, 1991

Kaleb Cole, a leader of the Atomwaffen Division in the US, was convicted of plotting to intimidate and threaten journalists and advocates who were attempting to expose anti-Semitic groups. Cole was sentenced to seven years in prison.

Patrick Sauer, a freelance journalist, described, in his article in the Smithsonian Mag 27th August 2018, Holocaust survivor **Mel Mermelstein's** fight to prevent Willis Carto, author of anti-Semitic books and the founder of the Institute for Historical Review (IHR), from discrediting the Holocaust. During a conference, Carto challenged the audience to prove that Jews were slaughtered in the Holocaust. Mermelstein's lifelong work to remember the victims of the Holocaust and educate others on the atrocities that occurred was threatened to be discredited by such conspiracy theories, and so he confronted the IHR via media channels. The IHR responded by daring Mermelstein to prove that it did happen. They wanted Mermelstein to present it as evidence in a US court. If Mermelstein refused the offer, then it would be concluded that there was no evidence. Despite Jewish communities suggesting that he ignore it, Mermelstein refused to be discredited and sought legal help from the attorney **William John Cox**. With Cox's incredible knowledge of the legal system and Mermelstein's testimony of accounts, they were able to show that the IHR had breached the contract they made regarding their offer of money to anyone who could prove the events of the Holocaust, as a result, Cox and Mermelstein were able to go further and to win a case, after a considerable battle, for injurious denial of *established fact*. This resulted in Judge Thomas Johnson's judicial notice that the Holocaust was indisputable and was established as fact. Evidence perpetuating Holocaust denial can no longer be accepted in the court (Smithsonian Mag, 2018).

There is constant talk in the news about immigration. In particular, the ill portrayal of countries that are believed to not take as many refugees will have a negative impact on the community. Inviting the public to share their opinion on the radio can seem like an innovative idea. However, differing ideas, sometimes ill informed, the opportunity to share those views publicly can then lead to negative consequences. People may be encouraged to follow negative views, or it may validate their own negative feelings on a topic. For example, in the 2016 presidential election race, members of the public were asked to share, in quick interviews, who they would be voting for and why they felt it was right. This causes a butterfly effect, leading to a democratic vote being less than democratic, particularly when voters are not prepared to research for themselves and truly understand why they are voting. Negative feelings spread further than positivity in an already disgruntled population. Statements are twisted to suit agendas; social media platforms allow inaccurate information to spread and video sharing sites are popular tools with younger generations to spread misinformation.

The Ku Klux Klan

The Ku Klux Klan is an infamous group of white supremacists who have terrorised Black people since its inception. It was founded in 1865, at the end of the American Civil war when the 13th Amendment was coming into force. Racial tensions were high with the disbandment of the Confederate Army and moves towards equality for Black people under the reconstruction of America. The 13th Amendment was passed by Congress on the 31st of January 1865 and was ratified on the 6th of December of the same year. It would abolish slavery across the US. The KKK, was initially set up in Pulaski, Tennessee, by a group of opposing resistance veterans. The secretive institution grew rapidly, despite various attempts to disband it.

General Nathan Bedford Forrest became the first 'Grand Wizard' of the Ku Klux Klan in 1867 and in 1868, the organisation's principles were published. In 1864, prior to the Klan's formation, Forrest had been a significant figure in the American Civil War, especially during the Fort Pillow massacre where nearly 200 Black troops were killed in protest to the North recruiting Black soldiers. Forrest lost a substantial amount of income following the Reconstruction. He, among others, had used a sizable proportion of his finances during the war. Being a cotton plantation owner, he needed the benefits of labour that slavery brought to him, and so, his income was significantly reduced. The Ku Klux Klan was formed by people like Forrest who were part of the Southern resistance and were set to lose out financially under the Reconstruction period. Forrest attempted to disband the KKK following acts of extreme violence toward Republicans, both Black and White. He stepped down as 'Grand Wizard' in 1869.

One example of the heinous violence incited by the KKK, was the Union County lynchings. During January and February of 1865, 12 Black men were taken from jail and killed by KKK members.

The Klan continued to grow throughout the late 1860s and 1870s. Nearly all White Southern resistance states had a chapter of the KKK. Through intimidation and violence, members led a tireless campaign against both White and Black Republican leaders as they wanted to reestablish white supremacist leadership. On the 9th of July 1868, the 14th Amendment was passed and ratified two years later. This amendment secured citizenship for any person, including Black people, who were born in the United States, or who had already been naturalized (by way of slavery). This provided the security of equal protection for all citizens. Reacting to the 14th Amendment, in Mississippi and South Carolina, black codes were introduced which included laws for vagrancy where if a Black man did not have a job that was approved by White people, then they would be convicted of vagrancy. This allowed 'legal slavery' to continue as Black criminals were forced to work off their fines that they could not afford to pay. Consequently, there was a rise in Black people being falsely accused of crimes in order for plantation owners to obtain free labour. Juries were all White and those incarcerated were predominately Black. This unjust imbalance continues today.

In February 1869, Daniel Blue testified against the Klan for racial violence in Moore County, which then resulted in the violent murder of his pregnant wife and their children at their home.

In 1870, the 15th Amendment secured the right for Black Americans to vote. However, particularly in the South, state practices prevented Black men from voting by requiring them to pay taxes, or to be able to read and write as well as other limitations. Black Americans struggled to access education and higher-level work. This inequality of citizen status became more prominent as the Jim Crow laws and black codes came into force from 1877. These laws legitimized racism toward Black people and were supported by various 'experts' in academia, religion, and culture. Black people, fearful of the consequences, were compliant with the codes.

Politicians who supported these laws suggested that integration would lead to interracial relationships and mixed-race children and would destroy America. This incited fear in the White population which resulted in segregation, the oppression of Black people's rights and social standing, and negative stereotyping by the media. These divides were argued to be against the 15th Amendment; however, this was undermined by the Supreme Court in 1896. On the 7th of June 1892, Homer A. Plessy, who was mixed race but whose skin was noticeably light, almost white, had sat in the Whites-only carriage on the railway and was arrested. The Supreme Court voted that Louisiana's Jim Crow train segregation rules did not violate the equality of Black people, and therefore could remain legally. This was because the separate carriages were of equal measure with regard to quality, facilities etc. And so, white, and black train carriages were kept. Black people were given 'equal' access to facilities – however there was a gross difference in the facilities available to Black people versus White people. (For further discussion see Chapter 4 on Institutional Racism).

Revival Number One

The Klu Klux Klan's activities began to fizzle out once the Reconstruction period was over and as Jim Crow laws were introduced and accepted by White people as the norm. However, it was revived over several years due to increased immigration, with its membership peaking in 1920. The outlook for the KKK changed as their attentions shifted towards immigration, but their racist views of Black

Americans remained. The 1920s saw North and Midwest middle class protestants agreeing with the principles of the KKK as they feared that America's traditional culture would change with the arrival of people from abroad. The 1915 film 'Birth of a Nation', directed by D. W. Griffiths, inspired the Klan revival as it was a nationalist film invoking emotion and subsequent action surrounding the depicted presidential assassination. The KKK remained secretive, and members disguised their identities with white hoods and robes that were sold to new members. The organisation began to accumulate large funds, which it used to fund protests on topics such as immigration, the League of Nations, foreign policy, and alcohol prohibition. The Klan blamed consumerism on the Jews and used the stereotype of Jewish bankers as fuel. They opposed Catholic schools and managed to ban them in Oregon. The Klan gained media attention and although coverage was often negative, this inadvertently attracted more members. Mass rallies took place with hundreds of thousands of Klan members in attendance, as well as ceremonial cross burnings. This initial revival came to an abrupt decline as the leadership disintegrated for several reasons, including scandals, arrests, and disregard for the morals of the organisation.

Revival Number Two

KKK activity increased again during the 1950s and 60s with the peak of the civil rights movement. As Black and Hispanic people were given more rights, the KKK began to grow in numbers again. They fought against the desegregation movement by parading at night, hosting large rallies, and intimating Black people. Their members included government officials and police officers which meant that the Klan activities were difficult to prevent. KKK protests and rallies intensified, there were drive-by shootings in Black communities, Freedom Riders' buses were bombed, and activists were beaten.

In 1957, a Black handyman named Judge Edward Aaron was approached by six hooded KKK members while he was walking with a female companion in Birmingham, Alabama. He was knocked unconscious, abducted, beaten, castrated, and was taken to a creek where he was left to die. Aaron unexpectedly survived and testified against his attackers. Two of them testified against the other four and were given five years in prison for their involvement. The other four were sentenced to 20 years in prison. However, George Wallace, who became the new Governor of Alabama, pardoned those four men. The other two were not pardoned despite their cooperation with law officials during the investigation.

In 1963, Sixteenth Street Baptist Church was bombed by the KKK killing four people and injuring many more. In 1977, a white supremacist who was the conspirator to the bombing Robert Edward Chambliss was convicted.

In 1964, the Mississippi chapter of the KKK firebombed twenty churches whose congregation was predominately Black. Three civil rights activists, Michael Henry Schwerner, James Earl Chaney and Andrew Goodman, were also killed. Edgar Ray Killen was only convicted of their murder 41 years later in 2005. Also, in 1964, KKK member James

Seale kidnapped and murdered two African American men from Mississippi named Henry Dee and Charles Moore. After Seale and others brutally beat the men, they weighed them down with rocks and threw them into the river to drown. 40 years later in 2007, Seale was convicted of their murders. Following this conviction, the Emmett Till Unsolved Civil Rights Crime Act 2007 was announced, named after the murder of Emmett Till from 1955 which highlighted the legal injustice involved in the civil rights violence.

On the 10th of January 1966, KKK members in two cars pulled up to the home of an African American activist, Vernon Dahmer. Dahmer and his family were asleep when the Klansmen set their home and the store, they owned alight and shot through the walls of their home. Dahmer fired his gun at the group of men who then fled allowing the family to escape. Sadly, Dahmer died later from the burns he had sustained.

Louis Beams was key to the KKK movement in the 70s and 80s. Beams was born in 1946 and served in the Vietnamese War for 18 months before returning to America with a hatred for the Vietnamese and Communism.

Beam was arrested in the 1970s for the Pacifica radio station bombing of KPFT radio station in 1970, and for a shooting at a Communist party headquarters, the Greensboro Massacre of 1979. Charges were dropped on both counts. 'There was a disagreement regarding the fishing of shrimp between the Vietnamese fishermen and the local commercial fishermen. The KKK attacked the homes and boats of the Vietnamese. In 1983, Beam authored the essay 'New World Order' about America's free men and confronting the police, propaganda to follow him and David Duke, the founder of the Knights of the Ku Klux Klan. Beam was working up the ranks and was good at training new members, as well as recruiting for them. Beam formed allegiances with a man named Richard Butler, who along with others, had formed The Order, a domestic extremism group. Copies of Beam's essay was distributed among its members. Beam was using the digital world to begin to promote White supremacy, using new internet technology to create forums for like-minded people. Beam was arrested after he had fled to Mexico in 1987 but was cleared of sedition charges by an all-White jury. He went on to release further white supremacist materials, and suggested to the members that it would be easier to avoid large organisations, setting up smaller and individual cells to avoid being apprehended by officials.

In the 1970s, David Duke became the KKK's Grand Wizard. He also had strong antisemitic views. In the late 80s, David Duke ran for senate and later supported Donald Trump through his election campaigns. This was interesting, particularly after Trump 'blamed both sides' for the 2017 Charlottesville Rally, a rally created by white supremacists, where violence erupted, and a counter protester was killed. Duke was finally permanently suspended from Twitter in 2020.

On the 3rd of November 1979, an American leftist group gathered to protest against the KKK in a predominately Black populated housing estate in

Greensboro, North Carolina. Before their planned march at midday, eight vehicles, carrying over 30 men descended upon the group. Members of the local KKK and Nazi groups had come to the rally meeting point to shoot the protesters with an array of weapons. There was no law enforcement present. Five protesters were killed and 10 were injured within an 88 second timeframe. News reporters could do nothing but film the atrocity. It became known as the Greensboro massacre.

It has been said that the police were warned twice of what was happening that morning, firstly about the number of people taking part and then that weapons would be involved. It is believed that the message did not reach the shift commander. At 10.30am, the commander reminded officers that the rally needed to be staffed from 11.30am. The ambush happened at 11.22am. The convoy was spotted by an officer as it was enroute, and the officer called to check that the route was being staffed. He was told that it was not time yet. On the 17th of November 1980, the all-white jury, found the members of the KKK and Nazi groups not guilty of murder. In June 1985, following various appeals and lawsuits, eight defendants were convicted of being liable for wrongful death.

After this massacre, members of the KKK and Nazi supporters began to join forces to form new waves of white supremacy groups.

In 1981, Michael Donald, a 19-year-old Black man, was walking to the shop, when he was abducted, tortured, and hung from a tree with his throat slit by members of the United Klans of America. Donald had been accused of killing a White police officer but had not been convicted of the crime. Klansmen abducted and killed Donald as a warning to other Black members of the community. They also burned crosses outside of the courthouse to intimidate and give a warning.

In 1997, the FBI were able to successfully prevent a bomb plot at the Texas energy plant. The husband and wife duo, members of the True Knights of the KKK, believed that if they could make a bomb and blow up the plant, it would produce a poisonous gas cloud that would cause serious harm to people in the nearby area, including the local school. This was said to be a distraction for a large robbery in another area. The FBI were able to intercept the plan as they had infiltrated the True Knights of the KKK earlier that year.

The Ku Klux Klan publish the Crusader newspaper. It was overtly supportive of Donald Trump's 'Make America Great Again' campaign. On the 2nd of November 2016, *The Washington Post* detailed how Donald Trump denied knowing anything about David Duke and other white supremacists despite having had public exchanges with Duke. They also reported that Trump asked for a Black man to be removed from the North Carolina rally in October 2016 as he wrongly assumed that the man was a protester against Trump, rather than a supporter.

During an anti-immigration rally in 2016, held by members of the KKK, anti-racism protesters arrived to counter-protest. Violence erupted and people from both sides were stabbed, including an anti-KKK protester who was stabbed with a flagpole.

Arrests for violence related charges were made from both parties.

Far Right Movements and Splinter Groups

Far Right groups oppose the rise in immigration, civil rights and equality for people considered 'non-nationals.' They are often founded and largely supported by working class people who are affected most by the Government's socio-economic policies. Their attitude is similar to the attitudes of German people in the aftermath of World War I. Under the Treaty of Versailles, Germany was facing reparations, huge debts, and high unemployment rates, which led to an economic collapse in 1930, creating resentment, persecution, and revolt, paving the way for a new style of leadership under Adolf Hitler.

Acts of terror and racially aggravated crimes committed by White people are rarely claimed by any particular organisation, however all White terrorists hold the beliefs of these types of groups, and similar ideologies. Easy access to information, policies, forums, and online connections with others who have similar outlooks allows far right communities to reach further and further. When these groups fall apart or face internal disagreements, splinter cells usually form to continue the movement. Here is a brief overview of a few examples of the far-right movements from over the recent years in the UK and the United States.

The British National Party (BNP) (UK) began in 1980 as a splinter cell from the National Front (the 'new National Front') before becoming the British National Party in 1982. Founded by John Tyndall, the BNP has links to extremist and fascist organisations and has extreme right-wing views. Tyndall supported Nazi ideals on racial politics. The party has been known to deny the Holocaust and to be violent in their campaigning rallies. The 1990 deputy leader, Richard Edmonds, publicly declared that the BNP was a racist party. In 1999, Nick Griffin became leader of the BNP and in 2005 Griffin, alongside other BNP members, including John Tyndall, was charged with inciting hatred. However, Tyndall died the evening before the court date. Prior to this, Griffin and others had intimidated, harassed, and assaulted the Asian community and spread racial superiority rhetoric. In 2014, Griffin stepped down and on the 22nd of July, 'struck off' and 'banned' teacher Adam Walker became the party's leader. In January 2016, the British National Party were removed from the Electoral Commission. In 2019, the BNP's former director of publicity formed the Patriotic Alternative group. Mark Collett has used the slogan 'White lives matter' during publicity stunts in the presence of the Black Lives Matter movement. He founded the Patriotic Alternative, a white nationalist hate group in July 2019.

The Proud Boys (US) was started by Gavin McInness in 2016. He called it a 'pro-western fraternal organization.' They are primarily misogynistic and antisemitic. They support ideologies of male dominance including Donald Trump's vision of America. They involve themselves in street violence. In America, they have been officially classified as a 'hate group,' and in Canada, a 'terrorist organisation.' McInness is responsible for promoting transphobia. In 2017, a Proud Boy member called Kessler incited the Charlottesville Rally, where the group shouted Nazi slogans and chanted 'Unite the Right'. During 2018, the Proud Boys were present at various rallies that often resulted in street violence. During the Covid-19 pandemic, they spread misleading and incorrect information about the virus and the challenges being faced, namely conspiracy theories. In a debate with Joe Biden, in September 2020, Donald Trump showed support for the Proud Boys when he refused to condemn them for their actions.

Britain First (UK) was founded in 2011 by Paul Golding and Jim Dowson. On their website, they describe themselves as a 'patriotic political party.' On their website, they define a nationalist as "someone who loves their own people, nation and heritage." Their use of 'own' is an interesting possessive word when discussing the group's policies.

Britain First say they are against multiculturalism (they also describe it as globalism or internationalism), because they want to protect borders and keep Indigenous people and culture in Britain. Jayda Fransen and Paul Golding have both been imprisoned for charges of 'religiously aggravated harassment' including shouting abuse through windows. Both Golding and Fransen have been involved in Britain First's 'Christian Patrols.' In one patrol, Fransen carried a giant white cross and was recorded telling a Muslim shop keeper in Luton that Britain is a 'Christian country.' Fransen has also said that Muslim men make Muslim women cover up to prevent them from being 'raped' because men cannot control their 'urges.' She said this in front of a Muslim woman and her two young children. Britain First called the Prophet Mohammed a 'false prophet' and told people to follow Jesus. The videos distributed by Britain First showing the interactions are heavily edited, perhaps removing any obvious antagonistic behaviour from the 'Christian Patrols.' Golding was banned from entering a mosque or encouraging others to do so. He was jailed after breaking this court order.

The English Defence League (EDL) (UK) was founded by Tommy Robinson (real name Stephen Christopher Yaxley-Lennon) and Kevin Carroll. They created it in response to an incident in Luton where a small number of Muslim extremists shouted at UK troops during a homecoming parade in 2019. The EDL is a far-right group that is often referred to as an Islamophobic organisation by opposers of the EDL activities. They were most active between 2011 and 2017, holding marches throughout the UK, as well as in the Netherlands and Denmark. Anders Breivik, the Norwegian mass murderer with anti-Islamic beliefs, had claimed to be in cohorts with the EDL. The EDL later rejected having any formal link with Breivik. The EDL march in Luton on the 5th of February 2011 was their most attended march. 3000 protesters showed up, waving flags decorated with slogans such as 'Save Luton', 'No More Mosques', and 'Support Our Troops'. On the same date the following year, 2,000 EDL members marched through Luton again. EDL marches often ended in violence. They were not peaceful protests and were accompanied by a heavy police presence, resulting in many arrests. The EDL marches often featured a lot of alcohol, and the behaviour of its members has been likened to football hooligans. They have also burned flags from Muslim countries and accused Muslim men of terrorism and grooming girls and young women. Many protesters have been arrested and some were seen to 'Sieg Heil' – the victory salute used by the Nazis, undermining the EDL's insistence that they are different from Nazis. The numbers in attendance at EDL marches fluctuated before eventually dwindling considerably between 2016 and 2017. Both leaders left the party in 2013 due to their concerns about anti-Islamic radicalisation amongst the group. Various splinter groups have attempted to form since the EDL's disintegration.

United Kingdom Independence Party (UKIP) (UK) was founded by Alan Sked in 1993. He had previously started it as the Anti-Federalist League in 1991. In the 2015 general election, under Nigel Farage's leadership, UKIP won one seat in parliament. UKIP were very vocal about wanting the UK to be independent from Europe. Following several debates between all the political parties, the Prime Minister, David Cameron, agreed to hold an EU referendum. This led to the UK leaving the EU in 2016 following a majority vote. UKIP has denied that the party is 'racist' despite various problematic comments from members of the party. In 2013, one member, Eric Kitson, shared offensive posts online about Muslims two weeks into his new post as UKIP councillor for Worcestershire. Kitson resigned but faced no charges as there was insufficient evidence to prove it was intended as hate speech. Another member, David William Griffiths claimed that some people were born to be slaves. Pamela Creedy, another UKIP member, commented that Stephen Lawrence and his story was being used as a silencer to shut down discussions surrounding immigration and racism. One member was allegedly connected to EDL and shared some of its ideology. It was discovered that in 2014 James Elgar tweeted vile posts about young Asian men and also made sexist comments. UKIP members Ken Chapman, Magnus Neilsen and Robert Brown have all made offensive anti Muslim comments, while William Henwood has spoken about returning people to 'Black countries.' On the 26th of April 2019, Kate McCann for Sky News reported that in 2015 Carl Benjamin, a UKIP candidate, argued against an Asian lady who was explaining why it is not OK to use the term 'chink'. Benjamin argued that it is fine to use. Benjamin is a Youtuber who has confessed to enjoying racist jokes and finding them funny. Benjamin had also, while standing for European Parliament elections, commented that if he were forced to, he could rape Jess Phillips, a Labour MP. He is outspoken and offensive, especially on social media. UKIP continues to campaign against the Government's current immigration policies and vows to remove them if they are elected in 2023. Neil Hamilton currently leads the party.

National Action is a neo-Nazi, far right organisation that stemmed from the youth of the BNP members, it was founded in 2013 by Alex Davies and Ben Raymond. National Action embraced extreme violence, idolised Adolf Hitler, and the Nazi regime, had a hatred for Jewish people and had little or no aspirations for UK political representation, whereas the BNP began to look at censorship of the views, with hopes of political representation.

National Action had a huge online and social media presence. They would harass and intimidate anyone who opposed them. They held pageants called The Miss Hitler competition. Alice Cutter a NA member originally from Bradford – entered the competition with the name Miss Buchenwald – was jailed for 3 years. Their antisemitic, homophobic, and racist views are blatant. They have made Nazi salutes, displayed banners praising Adolf Hitler, carried out or incited violent acts on members of the public and have joined other far right rallies. National Action had extensive links to other neo-Nazi groups across Europe and the United States. Following the murder of MP Jo Cox by Thomas Mair, National Action praised Mair for the killing. Ahead of Mair's trial, Amber Rudd proscribed National Action as a terrorist group. Members or those who push support for this group can face up to 10 years in jail. Alex Davies was jailed for eight years for being a member of National Action after it had been proscribed. Davies and other members formed a new group after NA's proscription. The new group had the same principles of stress and persecution that National Action had. When National Action was disbanded, they moved on to the EDL and other similar organizations.

In the UK, members of a neo-Nazi group Combat 18 are now not allowed to join the British prison service or the police force.

COMBAT 18 (C18) relates to Adolf Hitler and where the letters A and H sit in the alphabet. Seen as the 'white revolution,' Sergeant Paul David (Charlie) founded it. He was jailed for murder due to an inside rivalry alongside other offences.

C18 mostly recruited from football hooligans as well as white power skin heads in the music scene. They are known for attacking bookshops that promoted left wing ideas, LGBTQ+ pubs and anti-Apartheid rallies. They were originally linked with the BNP, but the BNP split from C18 because of its extremely violent behaviour. The BNP would not allow C18 members to join BNP and banned joint memberships.

The C18 were supporters of White Aryan people who were inspired by the likes of the KKK and The Order, who murdered law officials in 1984. C18 believed in the non-White takeover theory. They listened to white power bands. C18 was dangerous as they attacked individuals. It was a working-class movement full of hatred, they were misogynists who believed that women were not equals - women were not welcome within C18 activities, they were meant to stay home and look after the children.

The FBI have been targeting groups such as The Base and Atomwaffen Division and have made several arrests in recent years. In April of 2021, Atomwaffen Division were proscribed as a terrorist organisation in the UK, including the new name of National Socialist Order. The Base followed in July of 2021.

Chapter 9: Mass Murderers and The Power of 'Blurred Lines' Justice

White males committed all of the following offences. There are very few known female mass shooters.

Some of these are labelled as being committed by a 'lone wolf' while others are described as a 'mass murder.' However, owing to the nature of these attacks and the reasons behind them, I believe that some should also be classified as terrorist attacks. These acts of violence were motivated by political and racial hatred which characterizes terrorism. For each case, the author has given a brief overview and outlined their understanding/classification based on the evidence obtained via public records.

James Huberty

San Ysidro, California, USA

22 killed and 20 injured.

18th July 1984

Poor mental health and an overwhelming 'down on his luck' attitude may have led James Huberty to slaughter 22 innocent people on the 18th of July 1984. However, his overt distaste for Hispanic people and the location of the shooting, a restaurant facing the 'teeming Mexican border,' indicate clear racial motivations. He was a supporter of right-wing policies, particularly those concerning anti-immigration. Before he committed the act, he told his wife Etna that 'society had had its chance,' indicating social and political frustrations. He allegedly blamed Hispanics for his own unemployment; 'they had the jobs he felt he should have.' The suggestion of a 'grand final gesture' implies that the murder of those individuals may have seemed like an appropriate outlet for Huberty's frustrations.

Huberty's actions were not only racist, but also xenophobic. This act could well be considered that of a 'lone wolf.' But should Huberty be considered a terrorist? I believe so. He enacted terror and his motivations were racial, xenophobic, and political.

Patrick Sherrel

Oklahoma, USA

15 killed and 6 injured.

20th August 1986

On the 20th of August 1986, Patrick Sherrel attacked the post office where he worked. The attack was seemingly premeditated as the day before he had warned one of his female coworkers to not come in the following day, showing some unexpected compassion.

Sherrel did not seem to be politically or racially motivated in his attack on his colleagues, and it has been referred to as a revenge attack. Sherrel had been at risk of losing his job following various complaints about him as well as reports of lateness. He had also told the Postal Workers Union that he felt mistreated. Sherrel clearly had an issue with his place of work. In the attack, he killed 15 people, including himself, and injured six others. The SWAT team that attended the scene tried to negotiate with Sherrel but were unsuccessful and by the time they entered the building, Sherrel was already dead.

Patrick Sherrel is a prime example of a 'lone wolf' mass murderer. Although he committed an act of domestic terrorism, the reasoning behind it was nondiscriminatory and his agenda was personal rather than political.

Julian Knight

Melbourne, Australia

7 killed and 19 injured.

9th August 1987

19-year-old, military obsessed, Julian Knight had been dismissed from military college just 16 days prior to the attack. He used three weapons in a 'murder spree' in Clifton Hill, Victoria. He shot at every car that passed him, using all the ammunition in the first weapon within just five minutes. Knight then continued to shoot with the next two weapons, shooting at a police helicopter that was searching for him, dangerously penetrating a fuel tank. On being apprehended by the police, Knight told them he could not find his 'suicide bullet.' He was arrested and charged with seven concurrent life sentences. He remains in prison today.

Knight had no clear motivation for killing that day. It appeared to be the result of his admiration and excitement for the military. He also claims to have been assaulted while a cadet in the military. His attack can be considered that of a 'lone wolf' mass murderer.

Michael Robert Ryan

Hungerford, England, United Kingdom

16 killed and 15 injured.

19th August 1987

The Hungerford Massacre was indeed the act of a 'lone wolf' mass murderer. Michael Ryan had no strong political views, and no obvious motivation for his crimes that day. It has been said that he was angry at the world. His targeting followed no obvious pattern, he killed whoever he came across, including his mother and his dog. The shootings took place in various locations as Ryan moved from one victim to another. He eventually accepted a position in the primary school he had once attended and continued to shoot at police officers as they surrounded him. As police negotiators attempted to speak with him, Ryan killed himself with a shot to the head. His attack was non-discriminatory, as he shot people of different ages and gender, without remorse or reasoning.

Thomas Hamilton
Dunblane, Scotland, United Kingdom

18 killed and 15 injured.

13th March 1996

There had been growing concern about Thomas Hamilton prior to his attack on Dunblane Primary School. There were reports of indecent behaviour towards young boys which ended his role in the Scouts and other youth groups which he had led. He was also facing business problems which he blamed on these rumours.

Hamilton legally owned firearms and used four of them in his attack on the primary school. He entered the school's gymnasium and began shooting the Year 1 class (5 to 6-year-olds) in there. Gwen Mayor, the class's teacher, was killed alongside 16 of her pupils. 15 other children were injured in the attack.

Hamilton then killed himself before he could be arrested.

With no political or racial agenda, Hamilton was a 'lone wolf' mass murderer who killed innocent children and adults.

Michael Morgan McDermott

Wakefield, Massachusetts, USA

7 killed.

26th December 2000

Michael McDermott was in financial trouble. He had run up considerable debts and had been told that the repayments would be docked from his wages. Minutes before he began shooting at his workplace, he had received a phone call informing him that his car was to be repossessed. He was also under police investigation for firing an armed weapon in a public place just three days earlier. McDermott owned an arsenal of weapons, ammunition, and even bomb-making materials. On the morning of the attack, he took three armed weapons and other ammunition into his workplace and went on a murderous rampage, killing seven people. Evidence shows that the attack was evidently premeditated, as in preparation for likely arrest McDermott had searched for ways to successfully claim insanity. At his trial, he told the jury that he was responsible for killing Adolf Hitler and six other Nazis, and had time travelled to do so. The jury refused his insanity plea and found him guilty of seven murders in April 2002. He remains in prison.

McDermott was a mass murderer, but he is not a terrorist. His motive does not appear to be anything other than personal grievance related to financial difficulties.

Wade Michael Page

Wisconsin, USA

6 killed.

5th August 2012

On the 5th of August 2012, Wade Page entered a Sikh temple and fatally shot six people during worship. This attack was clearly racially motivated. Page had multiple active links to white supremacy groups. He also played in 'white power' bands which promoted white domination ideologies. Page had been dismissed from the army for alcohol related concerns. However, there is suggestion that Page could have been radicalised during his time there. The Southern Poverty Law Centre reported that the North Carolina Army Base was 'a hotbed of white supremacist activity' (Marilyn Elias, *Intelligence Report*, 11 November 2012). Page was shot and killed by police.

Headlines reporting the attack described Page as a 'killer' and a 'shooter,' as well as being 'extreme right wing,' 'a skinhead' and a 'white supremacist' but they did not label him as a 'terrorist' despite the attack being racially motivated.

Frazier Glenn Miller Jr.

Kansas, USA

3 Killed

13th April 2014

In 2014, Frazier Miller, a white supremacist from Carolina, shot three people including a 14-year-old boy outside a Jewish community centre. He had a long, documented history with racist and anti-Semitic groups. From an early age, his father introduced him to propaganda from the National States' Rights Party, an anti-Semitic and white supremacist political party. From there his obsession with white power grew. His associations with the Ku Klux Klan led to his expulsion from the Army in 1979. He then formed the Carolina Knights of the KKK, taking inspiration from Hitler and the Nazi party. Miller organised rallies and marches to protest against non-White people. He stated that his goal was for South Carolina to become a White-only area. As the state forced the Carolina Knights from their racist actions, Miller created a new group, the White Patriot Party.

Miller played active roles in both the KKK and neo-Nazi groups.

Miller's attack outside the Jewish community centre was clearly motivated by antisemitism. His motivations, past associations, arrests, and charges, as well as the characteristics of his victims, class Miller as a terrorist. Miller was charged with capital murder, three counts of first-degree murder, aggravated assault and with the discharge of a firearm in a building that had been occupied. He claimed that he had shouted 'Heil Hitler' in the back of the police car at the time of his arrest.

Dylann Roof

Charleston, South Carolina, USA

9 Killed

17th June 2015

On the 17th of June 2015, Dylann Roof joined a bible group at the Emmanuel African Methodist Episcopal Church with the intention to kill. That evening, he sat and read with the group, joined in with their conversation and was welcomed into their church community. As they said their final prayer, Roof began to open fire.

Dylann Roof was the first person to be sentenced with the death penalty for racial hatred crime charges (*The Guardian*, 2017). Throughout his trial, he showed no remorse, sadness or even regret. He did not apologise for his crimes and attempted to cut witness statements short by objecting to them. He claimed those who knew him lied in their interviews. He testified most vehemently against reports that his childhood best friend had been mixed-race. Roof told the jury he had not had a Black friend in years and certainly not a close one.

Dylann Roof is a terrorist however he cannot be charged as one. The only reason being is that at the time, there were no crimes that could be legally classified in the jurisdiction as domestic terrorist acts under the Department of Justice Legislation. Also, the definition of 'terrorism' is highly contestable which means it is easier to charge Roof for the separate counts rather than a collective charge of terrorism. Media outlets reporting on Roof's crimes should use the term 'terrorist' instead of 'shooter' or 'mass murderer' to draw awareness to this act of white terrorism. It is refreshing to know that this is being carefully considered in 2021, Joe Biden directed a comprehensive review of the 'National Strategy for Countering Domestic Terrorism' as the current threat is primarily from white supremacists with racially motivated attacks. Alongside the other predominant terror threats from anti-authority extremists.

The shooting sparked protests and rallies organised by The Black Lives Matter campaign. Protestors showed up in solidarity with the victims, known as the Charleston Nine, who will be remembered and honoured for their kindness and acceptance. Protestors have called for Confederate flags to be removed from general display following the massacre.

At the time of drafting this book, Roof was appealing the death penalty verdict by claiming insanity. He claims that while representing himself in court he was experiencing a schizophrenic episode. This appeal for a rehearing was later refused. On the 25th of August 2021, NBC news described him as 'a White man convicted in the mass shooting of Black members of Emanuel African Methodist Episcopal Church in Charleston, South Carolina' (Romero, D and Cusumano, A., *NBC*, 25 August 2021). Why was he labelled as this and not as a 'terrorist'? Roof recently began a hunger strike while in prison, which he stopped shortly after, as he claimed that staff is unfavorably treating him. Roofs appeal was rejected in October 2022, and he remains on Death Row.

Alexandre Bissonnette

Quebec City, Canada

6 killed and 8 injured.

29th January 2017

On the 29th of January 2017, Alexandre Bissonnette attacked Quebec City Mosque, killing six Muslims, and injuring eight others. Bissonette's sentence was reduced to 25 years by the Canadian Supreme Court in 2022 due to 'constitutional grounds. His defence team had argued that the crime was not racially motivated and that there is no evidence to support this allegation (*Canadian Express*, 27 January 2020). Bissonnette claims that the mosque was a random choice for the attack, and it was not intended as a hate crime. However, evidence from his computer search history suggested otherwise. He often ran searches for other mass murderers, KKK leaders, white nationalists, and Donald Trump. He also followed suspect individuals such as conspiracy theorists. He allegedly stated to the police just hours after the attack that his attack was triggered by Prime Minister Trudeau's statement welcoming refugees. People who knew him told police that he was open about his anti-immigrant views. *The Canadian National Observer* named him as the 'Quebec Mosque shooter.' Even with a title like this, he has not been labelled as a terrorist despite his very targeted attack. Bissonette was sentenced to life in prison. Parole eligibility for Canada is 25 years, however the judge ruled that

Bissonette would not be eligible until 40 years into his sentence. In 2020, this was reduced to the standard 25 year eligibility time for parole due to the 40 years being viewed as cruel and unusual punishment.

Stephen Paddock

Las Vegas, USA

59 killed and 500 injured.

1st October 2017

The mass shooting carried out by Stephen Paddock at the Route 91 Harvest Country Festival in 2017 is described as a 'lone wolf' incident. The random 'blind shooting' of victims, a lack of evidence of any connection to terrorist cells or extremist political views as well as there being no racial or religious motivations characterise it as an isolated incident. However, in the state of Nevada, where Paddock committed the crime, Nevada Revised Statute 202.4415, specifically states that an act of terrorism includes any action of coercion, sabotage or violence that is 'intended to cause great bodily harm or death to the general population.' Under this law, Paddock could be classified as a terrorist and not a 'lone wolf' mass murderer, even though he was not racially motivated. Paddock committed suicide the day of the attack.

Robert Gregory Bowers

Pittsburgh, Pennsylvania, USA

11 killed.

27th October 2017

On the 27th of October 2017, Robert Bowers murdered 11 Jewish people in a synagogue in Pittsburgh. On the 24th of April 2023 Bowers was sentenced to Death. Bowers had pleaded not guilty to the crimes he is charged with.

Patrick Wood Crusius

El Paso, Texas, USA

23 killed and 22 injured.

3rd August 2019

Patrick Crusius is still awaiting trial for the mass murder of 23 people in a Walmart store in El Paso, Texas on the 3rd of August 2019. Crusius was arrested and charged with capital murder. On arrest, he admitted that he had targeted Mexican people in the attack. It was investigated as an act of domestic terrorism. Crusius has been indicted on 90 federal charges, including counts of hate crime causing death, the possession of firearms and the use of the firearms to commit murder. On the 10th of October 2019, Crusius pleaded not guilty to charges of capital murder. The defence team claim that Crusius had been diagnosed with neurological and mental disabilities. In January 2023, the Department of Justice for the United States of America reported that it will not seek the death penalty, however

Crusius may still receive the death penalty under Texas State law.

Crusius is a far-right supporter and had been actively involved with online forums that promoted White nationalism. Shortly before the attack, he had posted his manifesto on one of these forums. It included a detailed plan for the mass shooting of Mexican people, taking inspiration from the Christchurch Mosque shooting in New Zealand of Brenton Tarrant earlier that year. Crusius also cited the 'Great Replacement' theory, which claims that White people are being replaced by non-White people, as motivation for the attack. Crusius received encouragement from other forum users to carry out the act and to kill even more people than the Christchurch Mosque attacker. The site where the forum was located has since been removed, but other forums like it still exist and continue to be set up.

In his manifesto, Crusius stated that he hoped that the attack would scare Hispanic people into leaving Texas and returning to Mexico. Mexican authorities were debating whether to extradite Crusius to

Mexico to face charges there for acts of terrorism against Mexican people. Marcelo Ebrand, the Foreign Relations Minister for Mexico, argues the need for the act to be classified as an act of terrorism to prevent similar attacks happening in the future.

Parallels can be drawn between the rhetoric of Crusius' manifesto and President Donald Trump's speeches which incite racism and hate. Although Crusius has stated that his feelings towards Mexican people predate Trump's presidency, there is no doubt that the media's coverage of Trump's speeches highlight that there is some shared sentiment. A further charge is being brought to court following the death of one of those injured in the attack. This brings the death total to 24. For the federal hate crime charges, Crusius was sentenced to 90 consecutive life sentences to be carried out in a maximum-security prison in July 2023 following an agreement for the death penalty to removed. and Crusius' guilty plea. As of 25th September 2023, Crusius has agreed to pay more than $5 million to the families. A Texas court however may still impose the death penalty following a separate trial, however the date is yet to be set.

FINAL THOUGHTS

Throughout this book we have seen how political power overpowers the general population, transferring through different avenues with a range of speculation, perspective, and misrepresentation. Intentions and beliefs voted for via democracy, feeding selected information through from people in positions of trust and authority via mass media platforms to the general population, leading to resentment, hatred, acts of prejudice, violence, murder, and overall terror.

Racial injustice needs to be targeted within the justice system, not by those who enforce the laws, but by those who make the laws and policies. White terror groups need to be eradicated. By preventing the media from scaremongering, creating falsehoods, and sharing propaganda these groups could diminish. Likewise having racial equality in law enforcement would mean harsher punishment for these groups. Real publicised justice for victims of hate crime and discrimination would create a broad factual view of the climate, could create a high standard of education about the positive impact of globalisation, being inclusive and accepting of other peoples' cultures. We need to address the issues that belong with older generations faster to prevent further generations from inheriting them. Holding heads of state to their commitments laid out in their elections and ensuring that annual budgets are fairly distributed, ensuring enough money, security, and social care for every person. By doing these things there could be a decline in crime, social unrest, unemployment, mental health illnesses, and reduce the strain on public services.

People from the lower classes, with too little power about their own lives, use the media and the policy maker decisions to blame others. They often feel the need to make their voices heard but can use scapegoating to achieve a stronger reasoning to their plight. This can emerge in protest, violence, indoctrination, and crimes. In extreme instances, it can emerge in horrific ways. Ultimately, the lack of power a person holds means a lack of control over their situation, larger power privilege can and is often to the detriment to those with no power. If the power of the people were utilised in a fair democracy, with significant issues among the lower classes being resolved and less backing of big influential companies and states stake holders, the more crime and terror would decrease over time.

Oxfam published an article on their website on the 5th of March 2019 about Max Lawson who was Head of Policy Inequality for the charity. He noted how billionaires are always the winners in what he describes as a "broken economic system that sees wealth unfairly concentrated at the top." On the 16th of January 2023, Oxfam also reported that "the four richest Britons have more wealth than 20 million Britons" Oxfam are calling on the Government to increase taxes on the wealthiest, and to track their 'true' wealth that is often hidden via offshore tax loopholes. Will the power the Government holds answer that call?

On the 13th of October 2020, *The Guardian* reported that "ending world hunger by 2030 would come with a price tag of $330bn (£235bn) according to a study by the German Government" (*The Guardian*, online, last accessed 20 March 2023) According to Forbes magazine, 'Forbes World Billionaires List' there are 2668 billionaires in the world. Therefore, if the top 330 billionaires of the world donated $1 billion of their vast fortune, to eradicate world hunger, this could be achieved. If all the billionaires from the list donated the same there would be enough to begin to combat other socio-economic crises, without even affecting their wealth.

The top of the pyramid is filled with just 2668 people. There are estimated to be nearly eight billion people on the planet as of January 2023. There are trillions of dollars across the world, powerful people with the ability to make world changing decisions and 2668 billionaires, yet there is still hunger, poverty, water shortages, lack of medical facilities and homelessness across the globe.

Power, Control, Terror, Status, Class, Wealth. All the same things.

A note about the author:

Growing up in a rural, predominately white middle-class village. I have become aware of these indicators of widespread prejudiced attitudes. In pubs, private homes, idle chatter among people in the street and on public transport, conversations about the fear of a 'Muslim takeover' have partly replaced the previously popularly shared 'concerns' of the increasing Black, Irish, Jewish, Sikh, and Hindu communities. I have heard slurs, name-calling, insults and supposed 'jokes' about Pakistani people, Irish men being slow or backwards, the alleged handouts specifically for immigrants coming to the country. Since being able to understand the effects on other people – who do not have the same background and upbringings as I had – I find that it is truly astonishing that the level of bigotry and the lack of empathy that is seen among predominately white areas is unbelievable. I was blinded by other assumptions and ignorance and was blessed to be able to uncover a lot of discomfort surrounding issues about race, religion, sexuality, and gender. Recently, I have gained the knowledge and confidence to argue against these microaggressions and explicit Western extremist views. The reason I share this with you is because having a short but sharp wake up call to how ''we' treat other human beings has spurred me to research many aspects of social science, and so, my journey of social discovery continues.

Other Books in the 'A Toxic Society' series by Rae Stanley
  Children of Nightmares – to be released October 2024

Further books in the series will also follow.

Please visit www.raestanley.com for updates, or follow on social media channels for the most up to date information as it happens.

A full bibliography will be available on the website for this publication following the release date.

Suggested further reading recommendations based on the theme of this book:

Hooded and Backfire by David Mark Chalmers

Legacies of British Slave-Ownership: Colonial Slavery and the Formation of Victorian Britain by Catherine Hall

The Racist Mind by Raphael. S. Ezekiel

Going Dark by Julia Ebner

Stupid White Men by Michael Moore

In Black and White by Alexandra Wilson

Manufacturing Consent by Edward. S. Herman and Noam Chomsky

America's Addiction to Terrorism by Henry Giroux

The Uses and Abuses of History by Margaret Macmillan

Debunking Holocaust Denial Theories by James and Lance Morcan

The Myth of the Muslim Tide by Doug Sanders

Media Control by Noam Chomsky

The History Wars by Richard J Evans

History on Trial by Deborah Lipstadt

Writings on Media: History of the Present by Stuart Hall

Are we all Nazis by Hans Askenasy

Printed in Great Britain
by Amazon